From *Slant* to Straight: RECENT TRENDS IN WOMEN'S POETRY

For
the late Padma Tyagi
my mother

and
for Sudha Tyagi
--mother surrogate

From *Slant* to Straight: RECENT TRENDS IN WOMEN'S POETRY

Anne Sexton (America)
Margaret Atwood (Canada)
Stevie Smith (England)
Kamala Das (India)
Anna Akhmatova (Russia)

MANJU JAIDKA

PRESTIGE

PRESTIGE BOOKS
3/28, East Patel Nagar
New Delhi 110 008

ISBN: 81-7551-091-9

Composed by Praveen Sethi, New Delhi 110 063.
Printed at Chaman Offset Press, New Delhi 110 002

Contents

Foreword
7

**Legacy of the Nineteenth Century:
Elizabeth Barrett Browning, Emily Dickinson
and Christina Rossetti**
13

**Writing the Body:
Anne Sexton**
31

**Imperialist Designs and Gender Wars:
Margaret Atwood**
47

**Rejecting the Father:
Stevie Smith**
66

**The Many Faces of Desire:
Kamala Das**
83

**Poetry in Times of Terror:
Anna Akhmatova**
100

Afterword
116

Bibliography
118

Acknowledgements

I am grateful to Panjab University, Chandigarh, for granting me Study Leave for three years to pursue this project. Much of my research work was done in the Panjab University library, the American Studies Research Centre, Hyderabad, (now IACIS) library, and in the libraries of the University of Iowa.

I would also like to thank Professor M.L. Raina and Professor Isaac Sequeira for all the encouragement and advice I received from them, my family members for their patience and support, and Dr. R.K. Dhawan for helping in the publication of this project and giving a concrete shape to what began as an idea.

FOREWORD

> It is impossible to *define* a feminine practice of writing, and this is an impossibility that will remain, for this practice can never be theorized, enclosed, encoded—which doesn't mean it doesn't exist.
>
> Helene Cixous, "The Laugh of the Medusa"

This is a study of the major themes in twentieth-century women's poetry. It is based on the premise that women's poetry embodies a discourse different from that used by male poets. It has a distinct language with its own peculiar characteristics. The subjects it celebrates, the sensibilities it portrays, the tools it adopts, are all unique, certainly not the same as those employed by male poets. It has not always been this way. It is only too well-known that conditioned by the patriarchal social system, before they became conscious of their own voice, their rights and privileges, women writers tended to adopt the role inscribed for them. They thought, spoke, and wrote like men, believing it to be the only way. But with the dawn of awareness and with the spread of emancipatory ideas, they have woken into a realization that theirs is and must be recognized as a separate entity. The realization had its origin in a demand for equality with men, an effort to erase any distinction on the basis of gender. With time, however, the gender difference became a *causè celebrè* and women came to pride themselves in their *differance*. Their new-found sense of self and the discovery of the uniqueness of their individuality is reflected in much of women's writing in the twentieth century. No matter how far separated women writers may be geographically or historically, certain characteristics in their writings remain the same. These include a resentment of social norms that bind and shackle. This goes hand in hand with the desire to pursue creativity in an individual manner, independent of the male-dominated literary tradition: the desire to express the female unconscious without any inhibitions of so-called propriety or convention. Indirectly it is an attempt to set free the mind of woman, to liberate her from her marginalized position in social and literary history and restore her to her rightful place of importance.

Feminity, according to Julia Kristeva, is that which is marginalized by the patriarchal order. In the patriarchal set-up women are seen to be outside the "order," occupying uncertain spaces, often merging with chaos. They are allowed a place within the order only when they fall into conventional roles of wife or mother which do not threaten the position of the male in any way. Thus there is either a glorification of womanhood in traditional roles or else their denigration when they do not fall into stereotypes approved by men. Both these expectations are highly unrealistic as both fail to recognize that women are human beings, neither goddesses nor bitches but creatures of flesh and blood with ordinary human strengths and failings. Women's writing in the twentieth century, beginning from this premise, re-views the position assigned to women in their given socio-cultural milieu. It seeks to restructure and redefine women's roles in a more realistic, more balanced manner, presenting women neither as goddesses nor whores but as individuals who nurture in their hearts the hopes and desires common to all human beings. The feminist impulse in literature thus becomes a broadbased concern with the situation of women in the world. It explores the idea of womanhood and the importance of what it means to be female in what has essentially been a male-dominated society.

It is not surprising that an important concern of women writers is the indifferent status of women in society. To what extent are they given their due in a world that has either ignored them or else treated them as inferior? "One is not born a woman; one becomes one," says Simone de Beauvoir. The reference here is not to the biological difference of gender but the social discrimination that one must live with. In the traditional social structure authority was wielded by the patriarch, whether he was the father or the brother, and women were considered dependent on them. They were deprived of their rights, their individuality, and even their voice to ask for their privileges in the mistaken belief that their male protectors knew what was best for them, and that what was good for the male must be at least equally beneficial (if not more) for the female. Women's economic dependence on the male head of the family, their ignorance and lack of education ensured that they remained lost in labyrinths of unending gloom, silent and unprotesting. They saw no light at the end of the tunnel so they remained the subdued section of society: in other words, they remained "women." Not "born" women, but socially conditioned to "become" women.

However, the twentieth century, as we are aware, has witnessed a change in the affairs of women. The feminist movement of the first few decades and its revival in the second half of the century has been partly responsible for women's increasing awareness regarding their status in society. Very gradually, the realization spread that women, too, are human beings, individuals in their own rights, who deserve to live with respect and dignity, not just as appendages to men. In this transition from ignorance to awareness one may possibly chart three distinct stages. The first stage of pre-awareness was that of silent submission when women quietly accepted their subservient role in society, convinced that male intelligence alone, far superior to the female, was capable of laying down all social laws and that woman's duty was to merely abide by them. During this period the authoritarian laws that prevailed were not only obeyed but also internalized by women. The next stage came with the gradual building up of resentment when the female mind started questioning male supremacy and social custom that dictated to them their duties towards the home and the hearth. And the final phase was that of rebellion, when women protested against all male oppression. This is how Elaine Showalter divides the struggle for female liberation into corresponding stages – the feminine, the feminist, and the female. The entire process was a long and difficult one: there were oppositions and hurdles mainly posed by the men whose authority had been challenged. There was a division of opinion in the female camp too. A good percentage of the women were reluctant to attack bastions which, in their view, had provided them security and shelter. But change being inevitable, the movement could not be halted and the androcentric social structure suffered a blow after blow from which recovery was impossible. In this long-drawn conflict women gained considerable ground and successfully undermined the male bastion. The twentieth century, thus, has been a witness to the change in the social status of women and the recognition of their individual identities, capabilities, and powers.

How is this change reflected in literature? In particular, how does this change manifest itself in poetry? Women poets, particularly in the twentieth century, fumble their way between two contradictory paths: one which patriarchal society chalks out for them and the other which their independent spirit yearns to pursue. This dichotomy necessarily results in a confusion of identities. On the one hand is centuries of conditioning which has molded woman into a submissive *housfrau*. On the other is the libertarian spirit. Sometimes it is the former that is heard in the poetry. But often the latter breaks all shackles loose to make itself heard. The female poet has to grapple with an age-old male tradition, she has to find her bearings despite all oppression, and assert herself against all odds. Ostensibly she works within the tradition, but actually goes beyond it, subverting it, trying to establish a counter tradition. Mimicking the phallocentric discourse, she subtly topples it to establish her own premises. But all this demolishing, dismantling, and then rebuilding, involves a lot of struggle. For this reason, a feminine text, says Helene Cixous, cannot fail to be subversive: "It is volcanic; as it is written, it brings about an upheaval of the old property crust, carrier of masculine investments; there's no other way... in order to smash everything, to shatter the framework of institutions, to blow up the law, to break up the 'truth' with laughter" [Courtivron 258]. An important task of the feminist writer, thus, is to destroy edifices hitherto considered invincible.

Women's poetry in the twentieth century is essentially "revisionist." The idea of writing as revision has been explained by Adrienne Rich as "the act of looking back, of seeing with fresh eyes, of entering an old text from a new critical direction" [Rich 35]. It means looking again at a given stance, examining it from a fresh perspective, exploring angles and depths that were neglected so far, re-mapping concepts and ideas, and giving them a gynocentric structure and meaning. It means that women must learn to be aware of the fallacies men have taught women to believe in; it means being aware that women live in a world which has been explained over and over their male protectors: by fathers and forefathers (significantly, no one ever speaks of "foremothers"). Women are taught to see it in a particular way. Their expectations are those implanted by the patriarchy. Their dreams, desires and ambitions, too have been handed down by men to a great extent. Thus has the male mind been nurtured in women, making them visualize the world in a given way, the way of their male forebears. This male perspective must be abandoned in favor of a more authentic approach. In the gynocentric scheme of things there has to be a revision, a redefinition of all important concepts, of one's needs and desires, of the world as it is and should be perceived. Such has been the feminist awakening of the twentieth-century which made its impact felt on women's poetry, too.

Take, for instance, the way men have generally treated the female body and its functions. They have treated it as an unfamiliar dark continent not to be approached, ignoring its definite needs and desires. Woman's body was a taboo subject to be treated only in terms of male desire and then it became an object of physical lust. This was the attitude passed on to women writers, too. Barring a few exceptions, before the feminist awakening, women writers avoided the subject of female sexuality. They did not bring the female body into their writings. French feminist thinkers of the twentieth century, however, emphasize the point that women, in order to be true to themselves, must write with their bodies and express the female unconscious. Helene Cixous calls for an "ecriture feminine" and Luce Irigary speaks in favor of a "parler femme" through which women will be able to express their hitherto suppressed unconscious and their bodily energies. "Woman must write herself," says Cixous. Her body must be heard. So far she has been made to feel "guilty" of her body; her body has been confiscated from her, alienated and censored. She must learn to think, write, and speak with her body. Consequently, women's writing in the twentieth century marks a return to the body. It is a return to the female body, particularly the body of the mother who replaces the oppressive father. The mother is seen as a source of strength, life-giving and nurturing. There is, thus, a revision of perspectives from a male-oriented one to a female one, from a phallocentric world to a gynocentric one. Earlier, when women were assigned a marginalized position in the patriarchal scheme of things, it was a monosexual universe. Plurality is introduced into it by including the woman's point of view, drawing attention to the contribution of women to society, and advocating a sisterhood among women.

It may be pointed out that Cixous's concept of the return to the female body has parallels with Lacan's thoughts on the child's separation from the mother's body and his return to it. But while Lacan's description of the phase of unity is a pre-linguistic, pre-Oedipal one, Cixous's idea of the return to the female body is a liberating one that enables woman to find her true voice and language. The "false" woman who represents patriarchal power and does not allow the true woman to exist, must be killed. An effort, Cixous strongly reiterates, must be made to inscribe the breath of the "whole" woman.

This study of women's poetry attempts a survey of some of the important themes and ideas that emerge in women's poetry of the twentieth century. Beginning with the contribution of nineteenth-century poets like Elizabeth Barrett Browning, Emily Dickinson, and Christina Rossetti, exploring the manner in which they paved the way for later poets, it moves on to the work of women poets from different geographical locales, highlighting how the predominant concerns remain more or less the same, no matter where the speaking voice is located. In the case of each individual poet, the effort is to focus on one main theme which becomes representative of a larger concern with the position of women viewed against diverse social and cultural backgrounds.

Legacy of the Nineteenth Century: Emily Dickinson, Elizabeh Browning, Christina Rossetti

Alas: A woman that attempts the pen
Such an intruder on the rights of men,
Such a presumptuous Creature is esteem'd
The fault can by no vertue be redeem'd.

Anne Finch, Countess of Winchelsea

Poetry written by women in the twentieth century challenges a number of earlier beliefs. The first pertains to the idea that the novel, and not poetry, is the fitting medium for the female of the species. It was believed that women, if they had to write, should confine their literary endeavors to feminine genres and write about feminine themes: love and romance, marriage, the house. Women were best seen as passive beings, as voiceless, mindless creatures whose sole aim in life was to look after the interests of the male, a task that would give them the maximum satisfaction. Another belief discarded was the idealization of domesticity and marriage for women. This was a corollary to the belief in the intellectual superiority and greater physical strength of men which best suited them for an outdoor life while women were expected to stay indoors and keep the hearth and home. Hence the glorification of female domesticity, love and romance.

The long road to the present scene, when one may come across a variety of genres and themes penned by women writers, has thus not been easy. There have been reactions and counter-reactions, but the graph indicating greater freedom for women in writing has moved up steadily. And yet it would be unfair to give all the credit for greater liberty in writing to twentieth-century women because one discovers that the seeds of emancipation were sown in the poetry of the nineteenth century. It was the effort of nineteenth-century women poets that came to bear fruit in the twentieth century. Amid the Victorian reserve, the few fortunate women who could write and also publish their poems seemingly conformed to the tradition but subtly undermined it. They seemed to write conventional love poetry that spoke of everlasting devotion but, at the same time, attempted to break out of the stifling prisonhouses of patriarchy in which they were forced to live.

Elizabeth Barrett Browning (1806-1861) was fortunate to have the support of her husband, Robert Browning, and could publish pioneering work that gave a voice to women's issues. Even though she wrote a lot of traditional love poetry of the sort expected from women (e.g. "Sonnets from the Portuguese") she also wrote *Aurora Leigh* where, through several assumed personae, she articulated problems peculiar to women in a social environment essentially unfriendly to them. The irony of her situation lay in that only with the approval and support of patriarchy – symbolized by her husband – could she attack patriarchal presumptions. Take a look at one of her sonnets:

> How do I love thee? Let me count the ways.
> I do love thee to the depth and breadth and height
> My soul can reach when feeling out of sight
> For the ends of Being and ideal Grace.
> I love thee to the level of every day's
> Most quiet need by sun or candlelight.
> …………… I love thee with the breath,
> Smiles, tears, all my life! – and if god choose,
> I shall but love thee better after death.
>
> ["Sonnets from the Portuguese," XLIII,
> *The Poetical Works of Elizabeth Barrett Browning.*
> London: OUP, 1951.]

Evident in this sonnet is the passive mood of the speaker. The passivity is that which is conventionally associated with women. The idea being reinforced in the sonnet is the immortality of love.

This, one may argue, citing Shakespeare's sonnet on "True Love," is not necessarily a woman's domain. However, whether one expects it from men or not, at least at the time Barrett Browning wrote it, it was certainly expected in women's writing which was traditionally associated with swooning sentimentality, everlasting fidelity, and constancy. An important aspect of the relationship highlighted by the sonnet is the total lack of any antagonism between the sexes. It gives the illusion that there is no power politics in a sexual relationship whereas in reality one may expect to find a precarious balance of power in *all* relationships as one party endeavors to exercise control over the other. Elizabeth Barrett Browning, internalizing male attitudes, dons a childlike naivete and glorifies romantic love when she pens such poems that ooze sentimentality, making gushing confessions of undying devotion to a lover. She is working within the claustrophobic confines of a conventional patriarchal framework, hesitant to step out of it. In *Aurora Leigh*, however, Barrett Browning drops the mask donned in the sonnets. Here she emerges from the façade and creates fictional characters who voices many of the issues which had preoccupied her all along but had not been voiced in her poems.

In the first place, *Aurora Leigh* is a stylistic and generic experiment. As a novel-poem, it is an ambitious attempt to venture into new ground. It indicates a dissatisfaction with the usual style and genre associated with women and a reaching out for more beyond the horizons. Symbolically, it is an effort at breaking down walls which confine a woman in its suffocating precincts. Secondly, the central character is, significantly, female. This again, is in contradiction of the accepted mode which generally placed male characters in the pivotal role. *Aurora Leigh* relocates the woman, taking her from the margin to the center. Moreover, the woman character is neither the angel of the house nor the evil other who is visualized outside the male order. As such, she occupies neither the pedestal nor is she the whore hovering about in the grey zone outside the main circle of acceptance. Sometimes one and sometimes the other, hers is a dubious positioning in patriarchy. But Elizabeth Barrett Browning handles this tricky issue by working out a solution.

The nineteenth century was a time when domesticity and marriage were the most crucial issues of a woman's life. It was for a woman to be projected as eligible for the marriage market; she was expected to attract a suitable match, and to be able to marry well. What men looked for in a woman was her suitability or unsuitability for marriage, and what women looked for in a man was simply materialistic comfort, as Jane Austen so vividly recounted in the memorable opening of her novel, *Pride and Prejudice*: "It is a truth universally acknowledged, that a single man in possession of a good fortune, must be in want of a wife." Elizabeth Barrett Browning was well aware of social demands and expectations. But she wondered at their logic and in *Aurora Leigh* questioned these social norms which saw marriage as the desired end for women. The eponymous character of the poem has the courage to decline the hand of her suitor and opt for the life of a single woman. Aurora, who is a poet, in many ways stands for her creator. But whereas the creator found comfort in the cozy dependency of marriage, Aurora takes a bold step to live independently, an idea that Barrett Browning herself must have toyed with more than once in her rebellion against society. Romney, Aurora's suitor, is a wealthy philanthropist who holds a respectable position in society. Logically, there should have been no reason for Aurora's refusal to marry him. But her choice is between domesticity in marriage and her vocation as a poet. The message that she sends loud and clear by turning down Romney is that one may live alone if one wishes to. One may remain single and devote oneself to one's career. When Aurora chooses the latter option not many in those times would have been sympathetic towards her. Her desire to support herself on her writing rather than be dependent on a wealthy husband would not have endeared her to many. It is a controversial choice that Aurora makes.

In this text that carries a clearly feminist message, Barrett Browning ensures that her character attains success in her literary endeavors. She also ensures that the complacent Romney, so sure of the position that his gender and money have bestowed on him, is humbled and undergoes a realization of his folly. Romney's wish to marry her is seen not as the expression of love culminating in marriage but as the covetous desire to extend one's power and possess whatever and whoever one may.

> Who tells you that he wants a wife to love?
> He gets a horse to use, not love, I think:
> There's work for wives as well,—and after, straw,
> When men are liberal
>
> [*Aurora Leigh*, Bk II, 100-101]

Aurora is not so gullible as to be taken in by false pretensions. Spurning love and marriage, courting a successful career, she finally finds her place and identity in the world. Her story seems to underscore the idea that if a woman seeks success she will have to turn her back on traditionally inscribed roles and dedicate herself single-mindedly to her mission, regardless of social demands and expectaions. But, going back on this stance, what Aurora ultimately realizes is that success alone is not sufficient as a prop to one's life. Without love and commitment a life is incomplete. Art, she realizes, cannot be produced by one who has not lived a complete life: "No perfect artist is developed here / from any imperfect woman" [IX 648-49].

Aurora finally goes back to Romney, now a chastened character, and marries him. Elizabeth Barrett Browning, thus, makes a compromise between female aspirations and social expectations. Perhaps she more than compromises, because in her marriage to Romney, Aurora becomes a conventional Beatrice-like figure showing the way to a lost man. Like Mr Rochester in *Jane Eyre*, Romney has been blinded, a physical as well as metaphorical state, and must be literally shown the way. Going back on her earlier notions of independence, Aurora comes to the rescue and takes on the role of the nurse and guide. Thus, although the theme of *Aurora Leigh* may be seen as feminist, it is sometimes taken as a failed attempt to break out of patriarchy enacted by Barrett Browning's heroine. In her struggles she simply lays bare the pulls and pushes operating on women in the social milieu of the times. Beginning as a rebel, she apparently ends as a conformist, returning to the very position she had spurned initially: woman as the angel. And yet some progress has been made. Romney has been brought down from his high horse of smug complacency and placed in a position of dependency on the very woman he had extended support to earlier. A compromise is worked out without placing the woman at a disadvantage. This is what the reader sees at the obvious level.

On another level, it is interesting to note what Elizabeth Barrett Browning is doing – as a woman, not as an author. Aware of the support that her husband had extended to her, and wishing to acknowledge the debt somehow, she gives a contrived twist to Aurora's tale to make it palatable to the male bastions of society, confident that she is not weakening her own position in any way. Paradoxically, by seeming to support patriarchy she strengthens her own status. It is a subtle game that is played whereby she lets other gender win, almost as though she were saying: "Right, you win. I allow you to win." Thus the strategy of yielding leads to a greater subversion than the use of force would allow. It ensures a peaceful status quo and a moral/psychological victory for the woman, in the text for Aurora Leigh and in real life for Elizabeth Barrett Browning.

So, although the struggle of Barrett Browning's heroine to break free is deliberately left incomplete, *Aurora Leigh* does occupy a special place in the history of women's literature, serving as a pointer: not only does it acknowledge the existence of a conflict in the lives of women, it also shows the ways in which the conflict operates. The author, through Aurora, is telling her own story but telling it slant. This is a style similar to Emily Dickinson who spoke of the turmoils within but in indirect terms so that her contemporaries could not fathom the depths into which her poems went. In other words, she told all the truth but told it slant. Her contemporaries read in them one kind of truth but today, when the poems are read, they reveal a totally different truth.

Emily Dickinson (1830-1886), like other women poets of the nineteenth century, had problems with her contemporaries because of her gender. The men who first had the chance to read her poems would not take her writing seriously simply because she was a woman. So, she did write poems, but kept it a secret from all but a few close friends. Besides, because she was a woman, there were a lot of subjects she was not expected to write about. Keeping these limitations in mind, she adopted a unique style of her own:

> Tell all the Truth but tell it slant—
> Success in Circuit lies
> Too bright for our infirm Delight
> The Truth's superb surprise
> As Lightning to the Children eased
> With explanation kind
> The truth must dazzle gradually
> Or every man be blind— [1129]

The task before a woman writer in the nineteenth century, as evident from the works of Elizabeth Barrett Browning or Emily Dickinson, was to subvert patriarchal norms while seemingly conforming to them; using the oppressor's language she had to give expression to ideas and concepts that undermined the existing power structure and established another, woman-oriented one.

One of the biggest hurdles that women poets have had to encounter is the approval of male writers and critics. How would a male reader/critic respond to poems written by a woman? Would he approve? Would he be critical? Or would he smirk with contempt? Take the case of Emily Dickinson who, like Barrett Browning and many others, lived in those glorious male-oriented times when woman was looked upon as a mere appendage to her lover, husband, or master. The duty assigned to her was to make babies, not poems; the rightful instrument in her hand was the rolling-pin, not the pen; and her place was in the kitchen or the bedroom, certainly not in the study. This was the prescribed norm. Any deviation from it was simply abnormal. Emily Dickinson, who refused to toe the dotted line, who chose to make poems rather than babies, was diagnosed crazy, or "partially cracked," as one critic put it.

This is the subject of one of Adrienne Rich's poem on Dickinson, "I Am In Danger—Sir—" which speaks of a woman's role in a patriarchal world. The reference is to the critic, Thomas Wentworth Higginson, who called Dickinson "partially cracked." Dickinson replied to him, "You think my gait 'spasmodic'—I am in danger—Sir—You think me 'uncontrolled'—I have no Tribunal" [*Letters of Emily Dickinson* II 409]. In Adrienne Rich's point of view, this "partially cracked" episode is symptomatic of the social malaise that women are compelled to live with. She writes about the kind of life Dickinson lived:

> Gardening the day-lily,
> Wiping the wine-glass stems....
>
> [Rich, "I Am In Danger—Sir"]

All the while, even as she was engaged in her routine chores, the poet's "thoughts pulsed on" in the mind. If at all they were expressed in writing, they remained hidden from the world on furtively concealed scraps of paper. The real Emily was not revealed to the public. This was a survival strategy as she knew the rules of the patriarchal world. Dickinson had strong determination and will power – qualities then generally associated with men – so she held on to her identity the only way she could, by keeping the private world of her poems to herself, away from the world. Thus was she true to her private aspirations while on the surface adhering to convention.

Adrienne Rich appreciates Dickinson's circumstances and is concerned with what Susan Juhasz calls the woman poet's "double bind" [Juhasz 1978] a woman is expected to limit her concerns to the hearth and the home, leaving the field of literary creativity clear for men. But the poetic voice within will not be still. So she is compelled to be both, first a woman in a conventional role, and then a poet whose literary urges compel her to write. A precarious balance is maintained between the two contradictory pulls. This situation arises because the social and cultural given compels women to accept and internalize social norms, making them feel apologetic about their private aspirations. If they do have some ambition, they feel the necessity of male approval. It was so in Elizabeth Barrett Browning's time and also in Emily Dickinson's time. It was not very different in the mid-twentieth century when Rich started publishing.

Critical and biographical accounts of Emily Dickinson tell us that, contrary to popular belief, the poet was not an absolute recluse. She had a fairly busy social life and was in touch with a number of eminent men from the literary field, journalists, critics and writers. One of them, as we know, was T. W. Higginson whose name has been handed down to posterity, who – mainly because of his nineteenth-century mindset against women's writing – did not recognize Dickinson's poetic genius. The point, however, is that even though Dickinson was acquainted with writers and critics, she could not publish her poems. Poetry was considered too ambitious for women: they were better doing something less challenging like prose:

> They shut me up in Prose—
> As when a Little Girl
> They put me in the Closet—
> Because they liked me 'still'— [613]

Loaded with meaning is 'still,' the last word of the poem. 'Still' is on the one hand a measure of condescension, the patronizing society telling the aspiring woman poet that even though she is peculiar, even though she is presumptuous enough to dabble in male activities like poem-making, they not only tolerate her but also 'like' her (sounds hard to believe, though). On the other hand, 'still' is the stillness of death: a comment on society which would rather see a woman poet silenced than allow her to articulate her thoughts in verse. This idea is reinforced by the coffin image of the closet in the penultimate line of the poem. It also signifies Dickinson's awareness of her talent as a poet, and that it was a form of death to suppress it. The conflicting parties of the poem are the 'me' and the 'they.' The 'me' is the woman and poet who is discriminated against by the 'they' who are law-makers of society, not named or specified but a force that the woman-poet must reckon with.

Emily Dickinson was aware that she lived in a milieu that not only took no notice of women but also treated women as objects useful only in terms of their service to men. In all other respects they were non-entities. This hard fact is, however, acknowledged by Dickinson with some characteristic good humor when she says:

> I'm Nobody! Who are you?
> Are you—Nobody—Too?
> Then there's a pair of us?
> Don't teil! They'd advertise—you know!
>
> How dreary—to be Somebody!
> How public—like a Frog—
> To tell one's name—the livelong June—
> To an admiring bog! [288]

This poem by Dickinson, which her male contemporaries must have read as an expression of self-righteousness, sets up two opposiing parties on a battlefield: the Nobodies and the Somebodies. As in the 'me' and 'they' of the earlier poem, it is easy to see the gendered basis of the separation. But, as one Nobody tells another, it is better to be a Nobody than a Somebody because, look, how ridiculous they are! The camaraderie of 'nobodies' is not defined in much detail by Dickinson, but it would, in the twentieth century, evolve into a sisterhood of women's liberationists.

There is, in Dickinson's poems, a turning away from all external "man-made" events, a turning *in* to the recesses of the self, the female word that is kept away from alien eyes. This is why, perhaps, Dickinson's poems do not speak of external events like the slavery or the Civil War even though she was writing furiously during 1862-63. It would seem as though the poet visualized war and other forms of public violence as the outcome of malevolent *male* powers, and so chose to withdraw into a very private female world beyond the reach of men. Turning her gaze towards the soul, she decided to nurture the inner world. This was her form of revolt: shutting out a world that tried to lay down rules for her. In her own way, Emily Dickinson was a rebel. While still in her adolescence, she had dared to rebel against orthodox religion and refused to go to church. As a poet she dared to innovate in style and form, writing a kind of verse that had not been written before, with short, abrupt lines and a lot of ellipses, capital letters and dashes, apparently playing games with words and phrases. Exclusion of external events from her poetry, thus, may be seen as another form of her rebellion.

Dickinson being a woman, was not taken seriously as a poet. The complexities of her poems escaped her contemporaries who either did not understand them at all or dismissed them as clever games that a lonely spinster played on the backs of household bills and receipts in her spare time, a hobby unceremoniously shoved into her apron-pockets when company arrived and the hostess had to take over. And so a poem like "My Life had stood—a Loaded Gun—/In Corners—till a Day / The Owner passed—identified—/ And carried Me away—" [754], with its strong sexual overtones, was not fully comprehended by the nineteenth-century audience. Why, it could easily be about an individual biding time, waiting to be carried away by Death. So, for that matter, could Dickinson's "'Twas like a Maelstrom, with a notch" be read in several different ways. On the most obvious level, as the nineteenth-century reader would see it, it spoke of the ultimate union with God:

> 'Twas like a Maelstrom, with a notch,
> That nearer, every Day,
> Kept narrowing its boiling Wheel
> Until the Agony
>
> Toyed coolly with the final inch
> Of your delirious Hem—
> And you dropt, lost,
> When something broke—
> And let you from a Dream—

It seems as though the poet is referring to death which is always there, always waiting in the wings, coming nearer everyday, slowly but surely. All the while, an individual waits, mesmerized for the imminent end. But when the end comes, one is powerless to act, almost as though hypnotized:

And not a Sinew—stirred—could help,
And sense was setting numb—
When God—remembered—and the Fiend
Let go, then, Overcome—

As if your sentence stood—pronounced—
And you were frozen led
From Dungeon's luxury of Doubt
To Gibbets, and the Dead—

And when the Film had stitched your eyes
A Creature gasped "Reprieve!"
Which anguish was the utterest—then—
To perish, or to live? [414]

A conventional reading of the poem would perhaps see it as the encounter of an individual with God or the Devil, the closeness to death and the union with God. Such a reading must have been acceptable to the nineteenth-century reader. And yet, when we look again at the poem, other meanings seem to emerge. The maelstrom, the delirium, the numbness, the inertia, the falling in a dream, the gasping, the "Reprieve"—all these may be taken as expressive of a sexual experience, a truth that the poet could only tell "slant." The idea conveyed in the final lines is that of dying at a moment of ecstasy, the oneness of pleasure and pain. But it is an idea that is conveyed indirectly, not directly. It is something one may discern reading between the lines. Dickinson, writing in the nineteenth century, wanted to tell the truth of her experiences, but could only tell the *slanted* truth.

Christina Georgina Rossetti, pseudonym Ellen Alleyne (1830-1894), one of the most important of nineteenth-century English women poets both in range and quality, even today does not receive her due recognition. Invariably she is described as the sister of the painter-poet Dante Gabriel Rossetti. No doubt, the men in her family had a profound influence in shaping her as an artist. In 1847 it was her grandfather, Gaetano Polidori, who printed on his private press a volume of her *Verses* and helped her embark on a poetic career. In 1850, with the support of her brother, and under the pseudonym of Ellen Alleyne, she contributed seven poems to the Pre-Raphaelite journal *The Germ*. She, thus, had the support of her grandfather and her brother without which she would neither have written nor published poetry. And yet, the choice of the pseudonym is significant as it tells of the woman writer's hesitation to take the centerstage in a primarily male domain.

Christina Rossetti, however, could not dedicate herself wholly to her poetic vocation. Financial difficulties led her to keep a school with her mother at Frome, Somerset, but it was not a success, and when her father died, she entered on her life work of companionship to her mother, devotion to her religion, and the writing of her poetry. Religion played a crucial role in her life. She was a firm High Church Anglican, and in 1850 she broke her engagement to the artist James Collinson, an original member of the Pre-Raphaelite Brotherhood, because he had become a Roman Catholic. For similar reasons she rejected Charles Bagot Cayley in 1864, although a warm friendship remained between them. When she was stricken by Graves' disease, a thyroid disorder that marred her appearance and left her life in danger, she accepted her affliction with courage and resignation, sustained by religious faith, and she continued to publish. Though she was haunted by an ideal of spiritual purity that demanded self-denial, Christina resembled her brother Dante Gabriel in certain ways, for beneath her humility, her devotion, and her quiet, saint-like life lay a passionate and sensuous temperament, a keen critical perception, and a lively sense of humor. Part of her success as a poet arises from the fact that she apparently succeeded in uniting these two seemingly contradictory sides of her nature.

In 1862 Christina Rossetti published *Goblin Market and Other Poems* and in 1866 *The Prince's Progress and Other Poems*, both with frontispiece and decorations by her brother Dante Gabriel. These two collections, which contain most of her finest work, established her among the poets of her day. While looking at Christina Rossetti's poetry, one must keep in mind the nineteenth-century Victorian temper and the repressive forces constantly operating on women then. Christina Rossetti was gifted with a sharp, intelligent mind but the keenness of her mind was suppressed by the pressures of social propriety. She lived a more or less sheltered life with little contact with the world outside except through her brothers and their bohemian friends. She was not well-read, unlike Elizabeth Barrett Browning, and remained unexposed to scholastic theories. Above all, what governed her actions throughout her life was her deep religious belief.

Goblin Market, Christina Rossetti's best known poem, has only in recent decades received some attention, and that, too, less than what it actually deserves. Formerly it was generally relegated to the children's literature or fantasy literature category. The reason for its neglect was partly because its main characters are two young girls and partly because Christina Rossetti being a woman, her talents remained undiscovered or under-estimated until she was resurrected by contemporary feminist critics. On the surface level *Goblin Market* is what may be called a "story poem." Loosely speaking, it may be placed in the ballad tradition. It is a narrative that follows a swift, racy pace, revolves around a given character and her fate, leads up to a central event, and apparently concludes on a (then) socially acceptable moral lesson. The distinctive feature of the poem lies in that it revolves around a female character, her fall from grace, and subsequent redemption. Christina Rossetti tackles a theme more ambitious than those handled by Emily Dickinson. In fact, as critics have pointed out, the theme of transgression and redemption in *Goblin Market* has obvious similarities with the ambitious project tackled by Milton in his *Paradise Lost*. There are, however, significant differences: Christina Rossetti's poem speaks of no male characters, except for the goblins who are not human but half-animals. Whereas Milton's epic speaks of the fall of Adam, *Goblin Market* speaks of transgression by a female protagonist. The role of a Christ-like saviour is taken up by another female character, the erring girl's sister. The central motif remains the same: succumbing to temptation, suffering as punishment, sacrifice and redemption.

As the story goes, there are two sisters, Laura and Lizzie, both young, innocent, and virginal, and vulnerable to temptation that lurks everywhere in the form of strange, deformed goblins who appear as fruit-sellers to seduce and destroy the innocence of unsuspecting girls. The goblins are fearsome, yet fascinating. One of the sisters, Laura, finds herself drawn to them despite her sibling's admonishments. Then comes Laura's transgression: she partakes of the goblins' fruit, paying for them with a symbolic lock of her golden hair, and returns home satiated. And then a change comes over the errant girl who starts pining for more fruit. However, she can no longer hear the goblins' call and realizes that her desire for more fruit from the goblins would never be satisfied and that she is now doomed to a life of frustrated desire, pining forevermore. Realizing that Laura is now heading for a fate as miserable as that of a certain Jeanie who had suffered and died for the same reason, Lizzie decides to save her somehow, so she goes to the goblin men to buy some fruit. When they insist that she should eat the fruit in their presence, she refuses to do so. Thereupon they are enraged and attack her with the fruit, trying to force her to eat. Lizzie stands stoically, braving their assaults and is covered with juices. In that dishevelled state, drenched with fruit-juices, she runs home and tells Laura to lick the juices off her. The ailing sister does so, and is saved.

This is the narrative on the obvious level. Writing in times when women were supposed to be goddesses beyond reproach placed on a pedestal of domesticity, it appears as though Christina Rossetti is reinforcing the Victorian ideal of womanhood. Laura is innocent and happy as long as she remains within the confines of domesticity, away from temptations of the outside world, particularly temptations related to female desire. Accepting the norms laid down by society, she may ensure for herself a trouble-free existence. However, when she breaks the social taboo, she has to suffer. Lizzie, who admonishes her from time to time, acts as the moral voice of her times, repeating the socially correct message.

The two sisters of the poem, it has often been argued, may be taken to represent two sides of the poet: one stern, self-denying and ascetic, the other sensuous, hedonistic, and self-indulgent. Lizzie represents the society with its repressive norms while Laura is the rebel, questioning and transgressing those norms. In keeping with the Victorian ideology, Laura suffers because she breaks the rules. She pays a heavy price for not observing the moral code. And when she regains life and vitality through her sister by symbolically "eating" her, she is in a way accepting the moral code, reconciling to the social norms she had earlier transgressed. Consequently, she can be happy once more.

The goblins of *Goblin Market* seem to represent the male world and a feminist reading of the poem would take it as an attack on patriarchy. Their appearance is sinister, they inhabit a glen – a shady, mysterious place – and only emerge in the dark, after sundown. Theirs is a forbidden world into which maidens may stray only at the risk of their lives. They are merchants engaged in selling fruit that is not normal or seasonal, but enchanted: fruit which has a disastrous effect on anyone (any girl) who eats it. This fruit is given not at an honest price, but for a lock of hair (to Laura) or forcibly thrust (so attempted in Lizzie's case). The girls are either helplessly caught in the game the goblins play (Laura, Jeanie) or else they, like Lizzie, must remain strong and ward them off.

Some critics, referring to the poet's personal life and her rejection of men and marriage, read the poem as an expression of Christina Rossetti's underlying fear of sexuality. The goblins, in their evil, distorted guise, represent the latent fear of men that Christina Rossetti probably lived with. This may be related to the fact that there are no other normal men in the narrative. Even when, in the final stanza, *Goblin Market* tells of Laura and Lizzie in their maturer years, neither their husbands nor their sons are mentioned. They are shown only in the company of their daughters and the close bonding between them is stressed. The concluding lines are:

> For there's no friend like a sister
> In calm or stormy weather;
> To cheer one on the tedious way,
> To fetch one if one goes astray,
> To lift one if one totters down,
> To strengthen whilst one stands.

These lines further strengthen the theme that sisterhood is powerful and make *Goblin Market* an unmistakably feminist poem. No wonder, therefore, that feminist critics discovered much to be lauded in the poem.

In Lizzie, who saves her sister from certain doom, Christina Rossetti portrays a strong woman, a female saviour. At the same time, *Goblin Market* presents the reverse side of the picture. Like the women portrayed by the other Pre-Raphaelite poets, it also gives us a picture of a woman who is weak and vulnerable. Laura, as she wilts away, is very close to the kind of women immortalized on the canvas by Rossetti and his followers. Christina Rossetti was far too conditioned by her social milieu not to be influenced by the stereotype. And yet, being an intelligent, thinking, person, she could not rest with merely the conventional portrait of a woman. So her protagonist is given other traits: a questioning mind, a spirit of adventure, and the courage to face the consequences of rebellion. Similarly, Lizzie, even through she represents the patriarchal order, is presented as an individual that one may not break: for instance when she stands firm as a rock facing the onslaughts of the goblins. Contrasted with the evil role played by the (male) goblins, she takes on a positive, nurturing role as she risks her own life to save her sister and nurse her back to health once more. For this reason *Goblin Market* remains a strong, woman-centered poem.

The poem may be taken as an inversion of Keats' "La Belle Dame Sans Merci" where a loitering knight succumbs to the charms of a beautiful woman who betrays him and he is doomed to pine forever more. Whereas Keats portrays a *femme fatale*, Christina Rossetti in *Goblin Market* portrays *les homme fatales* in the horrendous band of goblins. She is concerned with how men manage to seduce women and then discard them once their object is fulfilled. According to the conservative patriarchal ideology prevalent in the nineteenth century, women were attractive as long as they were virginal, but once "fallen," they were of no use and lost their charm. These were rules laid down by men (goblins in the poem) who were the lawmakers. The fruit, thus, is a metaphor for chastity, and the parallel between the consumption of the fruit and the loss of chastity is obvious through the poem. And yet the theme is subtly dealt with, in keeping with the Victorian taboo of female sexuality. Christina Rossetti, even though she tackles a bold theme, does not openly flout convention. She veils her point so successfully through this allegory that *Goblin Market* is often mistaken for children's literature.

Thus, in the work of Christina Rossetti, as in that of Elizabeth Barrett Browning or Emily Dickinson, what clearly emerges is the duality of tone. These nineteenth-century women make it clear that even though the rules they ostensibly adhered to, and the rules that governed the literary marketplace, were those formulated by men, there were unignorable undercurrents in their poetry that dealt with situations and ideas related exclusively to female experience. In their own separate ways, these poets spoke of the truth not just as they were taught to see it, but as it appeared to them. So their poems were products of the times and in a double-speak manner presented their creator's point of view which differed from the accepted social convention. In other words, they told the truth, but told it "slant." Doing so they made a beginning and paved the way for later generations of women poets who, in the twentieth century could, if they chose, remove the slant and present their version of truth in a straightforward, candid, unslanted manner.

Writing the Body: Anne Sexton

Write yourself. Your body must be heard. Only then will the immense resources of the unconscious spring forth.

Helene Cixous, "The Laugh of the Medusa"

Overwhelmed by the oppressive patriarchal point of view, woman has been made to feel "guilty" of her body, says Cixous. Her body has been, so to speak, confiscated from her, alienated and censored. She herself has been reduced to a false woman, *sans* body, a disembodied slave of the oppressive male and his phallocratic laws. Woman must recognize and accept her body, its needs and desires, if she is to become a whole, true person once again. Feminism aims at making women "complete" again, enabling them to accept their bodies without fear or shame.

When Anne Sexton started writing poetry, or rather when she started "writing herself," she immediately became a controversial figure. Why? The reasons are not far to seek. In the first place she was a woman who was trying to wield a pen. No doubt, the twentieth century had seen scores of writers and poets, but a new woman poet still raised eyebrows. Besides, not only was she a member of the unprivileged species, she chose to write about subjects considered unfit for poetry: she wrote about her lovers, her nervous breakdowns, her suicidal tendencies, her abortion, her menstruation, her uterus, and other such unconventional, even taboo material. Not surprisingly, the reaction of critics, male critics in particular, to her poetry was a combination of outrage and disgust. John Holmes, whose poetry classes Sexton attended, reacted vehemently, and started actively campaigning against her work, advising other upcoming poets to avoid her style of writing and to keep away from her baneful influence. Another critic felt nauseated at the sight of so much private emotion being exposed in public and was tempted to drop her poems in the nearest ash-can [Dickey 318-319]. In short, the patriarchal world of literary criticism was horrified at what was taken as a blatant display of so much of femaleness, from the sight of which they would much rather avert their eyes.

This reaction does not come as a surprise. The history of women's poetry, as we know, begins with women poets trying to write the way their male counterparts did. This emulation was not always a conscious activity: as far as they were aware, it was the only way one could and should write. Any other mode of literary expression would invite ridicule and scorn. So accustomed were women writers to patriarchal attitudes that they simply internalized them and followed them in their writings. Even if it went against their natural instincts, women poets chose a perspective that would win male approval. Not only did they consciously adopt the styles, linguistic registers, and attitudes of men, they studiously avoided whatever would incur the displeasure of the male reader or critic. This is what happened to Adrienne Rich who spent the early part of her poetic career trying to please male mentors, first her father, and then older male poets whom she was taught to admire. Only later did she become aware of her own voice which deserved to be expressed freely. Her predecessor, Emily Dickinson, was also a victim of patriarchal conventions and so she hid her talent from public eye. So was the case with a number of other women writers who were either unaware of or too timid to break the patriarchal norms in which they were steeped.

According to the conventions that prevailed, the universe of poetry was a phallocratic one that primarily focused on male issues and whatever pandered to the male ego. Among the subjects kept out of poetry was the dark continent inhabited by women. For the simple reason that they were different from men, women were considered abnormal, mysterious, alien creatures, irrational beings hard to understand. If at all male writers focused on the female body, it was only as an object of lust; they focused on its appeal to male sexuality and ignored its individual beauty and glory. Women, when they were mentioned in poetry, were either seen as mere appendages to the male definition of the self: appendages whose importance was measured by their relationships to the men who defined their roles in day-to-day life, their lovers, husbands, or fathers. Women were to be tolerated so long they remained within well-defined, uncontroversial, given roles–like that of wife or mother. In any other role they were seen as wicked or evil, as bitches or whores. For the men it was simply not convenient to see women as independent entities or even as normal human beings, cohabitants of a shared world. They were assigned a marginal position somewhere outside the familiar male sphere. Evident in this male hostility is a fear psychosis: a fear of unknown territory, of all that is different, or unfamiliar. Woman, as imaged by men, was not a flesh-and-blood entity; she was more of an ideal than a reality. In particular there was a definite fear of the female body, its powers, its passions, and its sexuality. Perhaps the male ego, in a way, felt threatened by the drives that give a woman her unique intensity and strength; it feared female sexuality; it feared the creative powers of the female body and chose to ignore them or underplay them by focusing instead on the greater physical strength and bombast associated with the male world.

In the early stages of women's poetry, too, when women tried –consciously or unconsciously–for male approval, one may discern a similar reticence about the female body and its needs. Groomed in the patriarchal tradition, internalizing male attitudes, women came to look upon their bodies with shame and guilt. It took a long time for them to realize that they need not be ashamed of being what they are; they need not be apologetic for being women or for having needs and desires that they wish to give expression to. Anne Sexton was one who had the courage to recognize what she felt and say it in her poetry.

Sexton's work stands out for many reasons. In the first place, it is intensely personal. An apparent believer in the feminist slogan of the 'sixties that the private is the public, Sexton chose to be deeply personal, autobiographical, and confessional. Perhaps one would call her concern with herself narcissistic. To some extent she is. But her concerns reach out far beyond the self to include all women. The themes that preoccupy her are of general relevance, even though they may not have been expressed so loudly earlier. Her work stands out for its focus on themes generally regarded taboo in poetry: madness, suicide, and death. These are themes that fascinated the poets of the 'sixties, particularly the "Confessional" poets. Poets like Theodore Roethke, Robert Lowell, Sylvia Plath, and John Berryman, among others, devoted much of their careers to the pursuit of such subjects. So did Anne Sexton. Sexton's poetry calls for attention in the manner in which it undertakes an indepth exploration of these taboo subjects, probing the polarities and the various contradictory aspects of the themes she tackles. For instance, if it is life she speaks of, she writes of its positive as well as negative aspects, the desire to live and also the paradoxical overwhelming impulse to negate, nullify, and destroy life, to seek a release from the burden that the act of living involves. Her poetry is also unique for what has been called its "flamboyance." There is nothing sedate or docile about her work. It demands the attention of the reader in a number of ways: through its startling themes and subjects, through the dialectics of its arguments, through its spirit of defiance and rebellion, through its unconventional attitude to life and to human relationships, its circularities, its ambiguities and ambivalences.

Anne Sexton boldly speaks of the dark continent inhabited by women, the territory shunned by male writers. She explores the deep "woods" and reveals its secrets to the world. As she announces her aim in "Kind Sir: These Woods":

> Kind Sir: Lost and of your same kind
> I have turned around twice with my eyes sealed
> and the woods were white and my night mind
> saw such strange happenings, untold and unreal.
> ....
> Still, I search in these woods and find nothing worse
> than myself, caught between the grapes and the thorns.

The woods, to Sexton, are not simply what men would view as the mysterious world of women. They symbolize the chaos and gloom surrounding the self, the world in which we human beings, and women in particular, live. It is a place of confusion suffused in a sense of unreality, a chaotic world in which it is easy to lose one's bearings. As Sexton's epigraph from Thoreau puts it, one only has to turn twice to lose oneself:

> For a man needs only to be turned around once with his eyes shut in this world to be lost.... Not til we are lost... do we begin to find ourselves. (Thoreau, *Walden)*

Sexton gropes around, seeking reassurance, looking for a sense of reality in these "woods." And when seeking reality, it is but natural that one should start with the tangibles or, to be more precise, with the first reality that one becomes conscious of in life – the immediate self. The rest of the world comes later. Only after one has understood one's own self can one try to understand the complexity of the external world in which the self is located. Paradoxically, only when one is lost does one try to find oneself. Sexton is trying to reinforce the idea that finding oneself involves turning one's attention away from the world to look at one's own self and its individual needs, to focus on the body, to that which is concrete. The body has matter. It also matters. It matters, or at least it *should* matter, more than anything outside its precincts. So, Sexton's search for reality seems to naturally begin with an exploration of herself: her body, its beauty, its sensory perceptions, erotic needs, desires, and aspirations. She invites our attention to the various attributes of the body and its capacities: its vulnerability to death and disease, its ability to feel, control, and reach out. What she seeks through her explorations of the body is the experience of wholeness, spiritual and physical well-being and independence. When this experience is shared with another, it leads to a mutually satisfying relationship, as in her poem entitled "The Touch."

Invariably, the body that Anne Sexton focuses on is female. While there are occasional references to male anatomy, there is little doubt that what moves the poet most, what she seems to view with awe and wonder, and what inspires her work is the female body which is portrayed in various states, sometimes in part, sometimes whole, sometimes healthy and sometimes diseased. As the critic, Diana Hume George, puts it, "The body is a vile vessel in Sexton's poems – a prison, a madhouse, a box of dog bones, rotten meat – but it is also holy. Sexton yoked the clean and unclean, the profane and sacred, *through* the body." [*Oedipus Anne*: 59]

Often, it is just one part of the physical body that highlights an important concern of the poet. Such a part does not necessarily stand out as a severed or disembodied item; rather, it represents the whole body, or even the individual in her totality. Sexton focuses on the hand, for instance, or the breasts, or the uterus, or other female organs which are not simply parts of the anatomy but symbolic of the female condition. These organs are then portrayed in their relationships with the outer world, relationships acutely defined through the various senses. The body establishes contact with the world beyond its skin by virtue of its ability to touch, see, smell, hear, and speak, as in *Love Poems*, where the attempt is to communicate with a lover. The poet sees this particular volume as "a happier book than the others.... In some ways the love poems are a celebration of touch – that's the name of the first poem – but physical and emotional touch. It is a very physical book." [Sexton, *No Evil Star*, 114, 117] The poem entitled "The Touch" concentrates on the hand which becomes a synecdoche for the person:

> For months my hand had been sealed off
> in a tin box.
> ....
> The hand had collapsed,
> a small wooden pigeon
> that had gone into seclusion.
> ....
> An ordinary hand – just lonely
> for something to touch
> that touches back.

It may be noted that the hand is a passive one. It is a recipient. It does not reach out or grope or beg for what its wants: it simply waits – waits to be held, waits to be owned, claimed, or possessed. It is viewed as a "wooden pigeon," an image that is more of an oxymoron, invoking as it does the free fluttering of a bird and the inertia of wood. The "wooden" aspect looks forward to the idea of the lover as a carpenter in a later line:

> Then all this became history.
> Your hand found mine.
> Life rushed to my fingers like a blood clot.
> Oh, my carpenter,
> the fingers are rebuilt.
> They dance with yours. ["The Touch"]

The two metaphors here are the carpenter and the dance of the fingers. The carpenter complements the wooden pigeon that was the hand, infusing life and vitality into it. The dance metaphor symbolizes the harmony and spontaneity of two entities in complete rapport with each other. It also symbolizes a liberation from the purely physical, purely material "wooden" state into a more spiritual, elevated condition, a transformation from passivity into activity. It implies that the body is not always passive. It contains dormant passions that may be roused at the slightest touch at the right moment. This passivity which undergoes a transformation may also be seen in "Love Song" where the body is "a boat, quite wooden" before the lover's kiss transforms it into something beautiful.

The passive body as it gradually awakens into a realization of itself – this is again Sexton's theme in her poem "The Breast" which celebrates the onset of erotic sensuality in woman. The entire attention here is focused on the female upper torso, just as it was focused on the hand in "The Touch." "The Breast" unabashedly describes the glorious awakening of female desire. There is no element of shame or guilt in this experience, only the exultation of pure joy, the desire to indulge in pleasurable sensations and announce the experience to the world. The awareness of sexuality marks the end of girlhood spent without any knowledge of sexual pleasure:

> This is the key to it.

> This is the key to everything.
> Preciously.
>
> .... the child in me is dying, dying.

The child is dying because the woman is coming alive. From a child the female persona is being transformed into a woman acutely sensitive to her body and its desires:

> Now I am your mother, your daughter,
> your brand new thing – a snail, a nest.
> I am alive when your fingers are.

It may be noted that the imagery veers between somnolence and wakefulness. Deceptively appearing as a docile "snail" or an innocuous, inert "nest" that may be used to perch upon, the speaker is actually simmering with dormant passion, ready to respond at the slightest touch, in fact, waiting for it impatiently:

> So tell me anything but track me like a climber
> for here is the eye, here is the jewel,
> here is the excitement the nipple learns.
>
> I am unbalanced – but I am not mad with snow.
> I am mad the way young girls are mad,
> with an offering, an offering....

Call it madness if you wish, says Sexton with a Yeatsean flamboyance. There is an excitement in this madness and Sexton is not ashamed of it because it is a natural process that occurs with the coming of womanhood. She celebrates the initiation into female desire, the rites of passage from girlhood to womanhood, and sings of the female body vibrant with sexuality, alive with erotic yearning and yet not in the least bit embarrassed about it. This is what critics, particularly male critics, were uncomfortable with in Sexton's work.

The body may, thus, be roused out of its inertia into a state of majestic glory. But sometimes it is afflicted with disease and then it becomes death-dealing. When she focuses on the diseased body, Anne Sexton follows the confessional tradition, like Sylvia Plath who waxes lyrical on a cut thumb or a high fever, or like Robert Lowell who speaks of night sweats or myopia, or like John Berryman who sings of an infected ear. Confessions are made when one is trying to cope with guilt, or when one is striving for an easy conscience, or for the purgation of the soul. They are uttered when one feels the need to rid oneself of all that is base or impure. Similarly, Sexton's focus on the diseased body seems to stress the need for making the body healthy, pure, whole and strong once more. It tries to purge all sickness out of the body which is the abode of the human soul. When the body is sick, or when a part of it is sick, it has to be made whole again or else it causes grief not only to the individual but to others, too. For example, when she speaks of her mother dying of breast cancer, it leaves her feeling guilty for the rest of her life, almost as though she were responsible for her death:

> On the first of September she looked at me
> and said I gave her cancer.
> They carved her sweet hills out
> and still I could not answer. ["The Double Image"]

The ailing body, thus brings grief. The mother's breasts, in particular, were a source of nourishment, feeding life into a new generation. They could create, or destroy, or both. As a source of nourishment they were life-giving. They were like two full-blooded ponies (as imaged in a later poem) before they became diseased. Implicit in Sexton's thoughts is the natural cycle of life: body growing to maturity, aging, then dying, its place being immediately taken up by another similar body, one generation dying in order to make room for its succeeding generations. The pattern, if we use Yeatsean terminology, is like that of the interlocking gyres, the primary and the secondary, forever expanding and disintegrating, each living the other's death, dying the other's life. "I talk of the life/death cycle of the body," says Sexton [Kevles190]. This pattern is viewed first at the individual level as the death of a parent, and then in broader terms as the rise and fall of civilizations, suggested in the imagery of the "sweet hills" that are destroyed and the wild ponies (which first gallop to victory and then gallop away into oblivion).

Sometimes, however, the sickness of the body is not real. It is dreaded for it has been so diagnosed. But, as in "In Celebration of my Uterus," the disease is not real and the body is actually clean and healthy:

> They wanted to cut you out
> but they will not.
> They said you were sick unto dying
> but they were wrong.
> You are singing like a school girl.
> You are not torn.

Sexton explains the origins of the poem in a letter to Robert Bly: "Day before yesterday they were going to give me a hysterectomy but yesterday I went to see some big deal specialist in Boston and I can keep it. So saved is part of the soul of the woman who lives in me" [*Letters*, 302]. In this "celebration" of her uterus, one may read a triumph of all that is female. It is an assertion of womanhood in the face of hostile forces, an assertion of the Woman over the male Other. The male Other is the hostile force that threatens the womb which is "part of the soul of the woman." In this particular case the threat comes from the doctor's diagnosis which has branded the womb (which actually creates and nurtures human life) as sick and therefore dispensable. Death sentence is passed on the female organ: it is to be cut out and thrown away, probably by rubber-gloved male hands wielding death-dealing phallic instruments like knives and pincers. But because the diagnosis has been proved wrong, the female force triumphs:

> Sweet weight,
> in celebration of the woman I am
> and of the soul of the woman I am

and of the central creature and its delight
I sing for you. I dare to live.

The poem is a re-enactment of the power struggle that carries on eternally between the sexes, the male forever trying to dominate the female, suspicious of their spirit of independence and threatened by their powers of creativity. In the perception of the male world, all that is female is "sick" because it is different. Woman is the Other who is not, who cannot be whole in the male sense.

Physical disease is symbolic in other ways, too. In "The Break," the broken hip is symbolic of more than just a physical break. Along with the hip, the heart is broken, too. Perhaps, simultaneously, there has been a broken relationship that the narrator/poet suffers from. Throughout the poem the focus keeps shifting between the heart and the hip, between the emotional and the physical, from the wilting red roses to bedpans for urine and stools. These two states of the patient in the cast, the emotional and the physical, are apparently independent of each other; sometimes they seem antagonistic towards each other, and yet they remain bound to the same mortal frame. Both are broken but the process of healing is not the same. The heart heals at its own pace which is different from that of the broken bones of the hip. The workings of the human body are complex:

This little town, this little country is real
and thus it is so of the post and the cup
and thus of the violent heart. The zeal
of my house doth eat me up.

["The Break," *Love Poems*]

In every instance, Sexton portrays the indomitable female will to fight it out, the determination not to succumb to threatening forces, mentally or physically. In "The Civil War," she speaks of patching up her torn self, putting together the broken pieces like a jigsaw puzzle to form a whole again. The God in her is shattered and must be rebuilt:

I am torn in two
but I will conquer myself.
I will dig up the pride,
I will take scissors
and cut out the beggar.
I will take a crowbar
and pry out the broken
pieces of god in me. ["The Civil War"]

What she seems to repeatedly stress is the divinity, the godliness of the human body: sometimes god and sometimes God. This is an overriding theme in *The Awful Rowing Toward God*, where the poet sees God in all the human faces around her:

God dressed up like an old man
staggering out of his shoes.
God dressed up like a child,
all naked,
even without skin,
soft as an avocado when you peel it.
And others, others, others.

These "others, others, others" comprise "a whole nation of God" as she sees them. The stress is on the extraordinary abilities of ordinary human beings, on the special characteristics which elevate them from the normal plane to a special, almost divine status.

The female body, in particular, is close to godliness in its beauty and in its powers of creation. This is evident in her poem entitled "Somewhere in Africa" which visualizes God as a tribal woman in all her glory, oozing health and vitality:

Let God be some tribal female who is known but forbidden.

Let there be this God who is a woman who will place you
Upon her shallow boat, who is a woman naked to her waist,
moist with palm oil and sweat, a woman of some virtue

> and wild breasts, her limbs excellent, unbruised and chaste.

This is an idealized vision that deliberately shuns all sickness and disease. The poem, addressed to John Holmes, ascribes to woman the power to steer the destinies of men and the strength to tide over all difficulties. She is the benevolent mother in whose care one may find security. Similarly, in "The Consecrating Mother," the Ocean becomes a mother symbol, a divine scurce of power and strength with "flashing breasts made of milk-water." The focus, again, is on the breasts which, in "Somewhere in Africa," were "wild breasts." Associated with them is a sense of abundance, the capacity to nurse, nurture, and provide nourishment to other lives.

It may be noted that despite the fact that hers is a distinctly woman's world, focusing on women's needs and desires, Sexton did not profess to be a feminist. She did not voice her views on the position of women or on the niggardly treatment meted out to them in a male-dominated society. She did not come openly into the public to champion the cause of women's issues or rights, nor was she the member of any feminist organization. Her concerns were limited to herself and herself alone. Others who came into her poetry did so incidentally, only in relation to herself. Caroline King Barnard Hall calls her "the last prefeminist poet" who "wrote her early confessional work in what was probably the final decade of this century in which a woman could write without being fully aware of feminist concerns" [Hall 82]. This, perhaps, is only partially true. While Sexton did not call herself a feminist poet, there is no doubt that her preoccupations are similar to those championed by supporters of the feminist movement. Her work shows an awareness of the methods by which women are brainwashed by patriarchy, the way they internalize male norms and attitudes, deliberately ignoring their own gender and its special needs. In the way she "writes" her body, she clearly bears the influence of French feminist thought. True, she did not indulge in slogan-shouting or participating in public demonstrations. Her poems speak about what it means to be a woman without, in any obvious way, going into the political aspects of the issue.

This pro-woman stance was acquired by Sexton only gradually. In the early stages of her career it was more important for her to please male readers/critics and she knew she could do it best by writing like them. As she confessed in a 1958 letter to W.D. Snodgrass, she was initially "afraid of writing as a woman writes." In fact, she admitted, "I wish I were a man – I would rather write the way a man writes." [*Letters* 40] She was apprehensive of what her mentors would say; she had a "secret fear" that Robert Lowell would consider her "a reincarnation of Edna St. Vincent Millay." [*Ibid*] It was still too early for Sexton to pause and wonder at what was wrong in writing like a woman, or whether there was really anything inferior in the work of Edna St. Vincent Millay apart from the fact that it was written by a woman. Her views gradually changed as her poetic endeavors received recognition. Soon the true voice of the poet, which was clearly female, uninhibited, and unapologetic of her sex, could be heard in the poems.

Having explored the depths of her person and discovered her own voice and identity, Sexton experiences the inevitable thrill of self-realization – the realization that hers is an entity independent of all support that had earlier seemed so crucial. And so her poems adopt a new tone: that of irreverence and defiance. She tries to subvert all conventional norms by turning them upside down, looking at them again from a totally individual perspective, finding in them much that is absurd, much that could be challenged. This is what she tries to do in *Transformations* where she retells the fairy tales of Grimm without mincing any words, without any euphemisms, and without any illusions about the lies with which we, as adults, feed our children. In these re-told fairy tales, too, Sexton is – although indirectly – exploring reality and placing it in the correct perspective, questioning the long accepted version. Again, the focal point of this collection is often the body, particularly in its grotesque or incapacitated form.

Sometimes the body is described in connection with spatial terms. Generally it is a house, the abode of the soul. Again, it is the female soul that Sexton is concerned with. In "Love Song" [*Live or Die*] we are told that it was

> the mouth that kept bleeding
> into the terrible fields of her soul....

The "fields of the soul" bring to mind the use of topographical images for the body by a poet like W.H. Auden. When Auden speaks of the body it seems to occupy a sizable geographical territory. Take, for instance, his description of the death of W.B. Yeats and the gradual cessation of life in the great poet's mortal frame:

> The provinces of his body revolted
> The squares of his mind were empty
> Silence invaded the suburbs,
> The current of his feeling failed....
>
> [Auden, "In Memory of W. B. Yeats"]

These images of spaciousness in Auden's work contrast with the confining images Sexton uses for the body. The fields of the soul are vast, but the body is limited to a narrow space. There is, thus, a constant effort on the poet's part to break away from all confines into a wider zone. This explains the images of flying, the wishful visualization of the self moving unrestricted through uncharted skies of freedom ("Everything in me is a bird..."), and also the repeated images of singing and dancing. The soaring body, the body chanting, singing, and dancing in gay abandon, is always female. It is woman's body which has the capacity for experiencing this wide range of emotions when the body and soul are in harmony, that is, when the movement inward is balanced by one directed out of the body. As far as the spirit is concerned, there is an expansive outward movement, away from the body. But the poet's attention can never stray too far and returns constantly to the physical state, the body being the locale where the physical and the spiritual unite.

When speaking of the body, it may be interesting to note the various perspectives the poet writes from. Is it the vision of the soul looking down at the body. Does the soul enter the body? Or does it remain disembodied from it? These are different perspectives, all of them are tinted in an ambivalent light. Is it self-love or loathing that the poems express? Does the poet hate herself as the evil Ms. Dog or does she adore herself? One is never quite certain. She seems to be caught in a double bind, sometimes loving and sometimes hating herself. Both these attitudes are reflected in her work. Do they contradict each other? It does not really matter, for these are human emotions which co-exist even if the one negates the other. They are negative and positive forces that may be found in all forms of existence. This is perhaps why she sometimes seems to celebrate life and sometimes negate it, an ambivalence best brought out in "Live," a poem that maintains a precarious balance between life and death, between the different needs of the self.

The body has to express itself and its needs somehow. It does so through language, and through words which comprise sounds: sounds that attempt to place some kind of order on the tumult that rages within the human system. Words are symbols of that which the system needs to purge itself of, just the way the body expels waste matter. In the psalms of "O Ye Tongues," Sexton speaks of herself wetting her pants and defecating – rather unconventional activities to be placed in a holy song. Perhaps her aim is to jolt us into an awareness of the shocking similarity between something as wasteful as human excrement and something like language which is indispensable in all human contact, but which is something that is expelled from the body with wind and sound. In any case, when a writer is striving for realism and naturalism, it is not surprising to encounter images of human waste in the work. The writer's voice is, after all, an extension of the body. Sexton brings herself in and out of her poems physically, as though she were lifting her body in and out of her poetry. If we read her work with this in mind, we see that through language she is actually displaying herself in various ways, sometimes as an exhibitionist, sometimes as a seeker of truth, sometimes as Ms Dog, but always, always as a woman. It is of woman's soul – housed in a *female* body – that comes alive in the poems again and yet again.

Imperialist Designs and Gender Wars: Margaret Atwood's *Power Politics*

Women of every race are the only discriminated group with no territory of their own, not even a neighborhood. In a patriarchy a poor man's house may be his castle but even a rich woman's body is not her own. Somewhere in our lives, each of us needs a free place, a little psychic territory.

Gloria Steinem

Margaret Atwood (b.1939) began her career seriously with *The Circle Game* (1966, poetry). This was followed by *Survival* (1972, non-fiction), *The Edible Woman* (1969, novel), and *Surfacing* (1973, novel). As a writer, she is nothing if not political. No matter what she writes, whether it is a novel or a poem, she repeats the same theme over and over again: that of dominance and subjugation, of survival in the face of adversity. But, even though this particular theme is foregrounded in all her writings, the effect is not one of staleness and repetition. For Atwood's concerns are neither narrow nor short-term. The range of her interests is far-reaching and varied. Nationalist to the core, she is concerned about the affairs of her country and its relations with the world beyond; deeply humanist, she is an active member of Amnesty International and raises her voice in support of human rights everywhere; and as a member of the so-called weaker sex, she champions the cause of women and fights against male oppression. Her sympathies, thus, are with the down-trodden and the meek, the weak and the victimized. Her main concern is the power game that is played in all echelons of human life, the politics that underlies all human interaction, that one has to take into cognizance in today's world. Power, whether it is that of a country, a dominant group or section of society, necessarily involves certain conflicts which have to be faced. The story that Atwood tells us remains the same, but in every re-telling it is presented afresh, with different nuances, against a new backdrop, and in a varied situation. The poet exercises freedom despite her self-imposed limitation and the central motif, the power politics between the sexes, becomes almost Wallace Stevens' blackbird, looked at in at least thirteen different ways.

In any given situation where power is distributed, at least two parties have to be involved and rarely is there an even balance of power. This means that one of the parties is stronger than the other. Inevitably, there is a tension between the two. Atwood sees this balance of power in a different light. The two parties involved in a power relationship, the dominant and the submissive are, to her, oppressor and victim. In her essay on "Survival," she explains at length the complexities of the relationship between them. Her main concern is with the role of the "victim." What is the victim's response to oppression? Is it a passive acceptance, or is there some kind of resentment or rebellion?

Margaret Atwood tells us that in any given power structure we may discern at least four possible reactions to victimization. The first is a complete denial of victimhood, a refusal to admit that the individual is dominated by another individual or institution. In most cases the victims are completely unconscious of historical or cultural pressures operating upon them. They internalize power structures and identify themselves with the oppressors. The second attitude is one of passive acceptance—the victim acknowledges being oppressed but takes it as a result of "an act of Fate, the Will of God, the dictates of biology (in the case of women, for instance), the necessity decreed by History or Economics or the Unconscious, or any other large, general powerful idea" [Atwood, *Survival* 37]. In this state the victims look at themselves through the eyes of others, seeing themselves the way the world expects them to be. The third possible reaction to victimization is anger—the victim's suppressed energies are released and an attempt is made to throw off external authority. The fourth position is that of the "creative non-victim" [*Survival* 38-39] when the individual tries to understand and analyze the experience of being dominated. Atwood stresses that the paradigm remains the same in all power relationships: "The positions are the same, whether you are a victimized minority country, a victimized minority group, or a victimized individual" [*Survival* 36].

These are the areas Atwood chooses to focus on: the victimized country, group, and individual. It is these concerns that are addressed repeatedly in her work. The country in question is none other than her own: Canada. Canada which has been overshadowed by its stronger neighbor, the USA; whose growth has been stunted because of the dominating presence of the USA; whose people look outward for success and inspiration, treating all national achievements as inconsequential; Canada, the erstwhile colony, torn apart by internal squabbles between the Anglophones and the Francophones. The relationship between Canada and the USA is an ambivalent one. It is clear that even if there are Canadians (like Atwood) who resent the inescapable influence of the larger country, the bond between them is unbreakable. For better or worse, they are bound together. Geographically, for instance, there is no escape. As far as the national temper is concerned, it may differ from the one country to the other, the politically stronger USA being more aggressive than Canada, but there is not much that can be done about these differences. They can only be accepted.

The relationship between the two nations is a one-sided affair. It is like that between the aggressor and the subjugated, the conqueror and the conquest. The dominant country tends to exert a strong influence over the weaker. As a result, Canada is forever focusing its attention on the USA, ignoring its national interests. As Atwood puts it, it is like two families living side by side, one of them, with little confidence in itself and totally obsessed with the other, is forever with its ear to the wall, trying to eavesdrop. The second one, meanwhile, is unaware of—or at least indifferent to—the presence of the former, being fully occupied with its own affairs. What may be noted is that the stronger country needs the weaker one for an affirmation of its identity and power. The weaker country may, perhaps, be under the illusion that it needs to define itself in relation to its neighbor, but actually is undermining or crippling itself, negating its own identity by accepting that of its stronger neighbor as the norm. This is a one-sided relationship, negative in character and consequences. This kind of a relationship is also to be found in smaller groups and organizations where power is not equitably distributed, where one party is dominated by the other.

Domination may not only be that by physical force alone. It may be a more subtle, psychological violence that is being perpetrated on the other, through ideology or propaganda, for instance. Political poetry of the 'thirties, particularly that of W. H. Auden, speaks of this type of psychological violence. In his poem "The Shield of Achilles," Auden describes a scenario where hordes of men and women who have been subjugated by the conqueror are regimented, dehumanized and brainwashed by the dominant ideology. It also calls to mind the oppressive regime of George Orwell's *1984* in which Big Brother monitors everyone's movements and those who do not conform must pay a heavy price. Tyranny of this sort is, perhaps, what Atwood has in mind when she speaks of the victimization of one party or group by another. Her poems are political statements on what she sees happening in the world, the ever-ongoing tensions and conflicts that inevitably accompany human relationships.

For any political document, there are certain essential requirements. These include, in the first place, an intense involvement in the history and politics of the times, an interested participation in the ongoing politico-social debates. Second, it must be written from a particular standpoint, a fixed perspective. Who is the speaker, in what context is the utterance made, and what is the viewpoint? Third, it must either propagate or oppose a particular ideology and be obsessively single-minded in its application. The nature of the ideology would vary with the standpoint and concerns of the speaker. It may be personal or widely-applicable, limited to fixed chronotopic boundaries or extending across vast temporal and spatial zones. Finally, it smacks of a reformatory zeal: the desire to either break up an existing state of affairs or construct another one, more wholesome, more desirable. This means that it would be critical of established systems and advocate instead a new system based on a different ideology. Throughout Atwood's work these characteristics may be found. Her books, her fiction, non-fiction, and poems speak from a fixed standpoint; they propagate an ideology to which she adheres unwaveringly; and she simmers with an almost missionary fire, the utopic desire to set things right, undo all that is wrong, and make the world a better place to live in.

Atwood's main concern is gender war, the insensitivity of the male culture, and the oppression of the female. She shares this preoccupation with a good number of her contemporaries and is very much in tune with her times. When she speaks of sexual politics, she tends to observe and rationalize. There is no suggestion of her getting emotionally unbalanced on the issue. The problem exists, she is aware of it, but it serves no purpose to rant and rave and weep. Instead, she adopts an analytical stance, approaching the subject from different angles, viewing it in all its intricacies, discovering that the pattern of oppression and victimization found in male-female relationships is present in almost every sphere of human life where interaction takes place between human beings on the individual or collective level. Take, for instance, what is happening all over the world in the political sphere: nations at war with each other, imperialist armies trying to invade and subjugate a weaker nation, organized hordes of human beings aiming at proclaiming their collective might by perpetrating injustice and violence on others. Atwood is concerned about these unpleasant aspects of human life and writes about them. She gives us scenes and vignettes, taking up slices of day-to-day life for observation and comment. Deeply committed to the cause of women, Atwood focuses on how women have had a raw deal at the hands of men, how their defenses are undermined in various ways, and how they are subjected to violence, physical, psychological, and sexual.

This concern with the gender question is presented from a fixed standpoint, through various frames, spatial and temporal. Atwood makes it clear that she writes as a woman, a fact that colors all the statements she makes. So the speaker in her world remains a woman and her perspective remains a female one. She is not interested in giving a dual-sided picture of the issues in hand: there are others who may be interested in doing that. Atwood is concerned with what is happening to women, what they have to say about it, and how they view a world which continually marginalizes their sex. As she once clarified in an interview: "Does the fact that we are women alter what we see? What we report? It has to, but nobody knows what the neutral stand would be. There's not [sic!] such thing as neither a man nor a woman. So we don't even know that person in between, what that completely objective Martian would say." Similarly, "the fact of being male alters what men say" [Van Spanckeren 232].

The gender question is related to Atwood's strong sense of nationalism. On both the issues she presents a female perspective, a woman's point of view. What, after all, is nationalism if not the desire to shield and preserve identity in the face of hostile powers? So is feminism the desire to protect one's dignity in the face of onslaughts from powers that threaten. For Atwood, the two, Canadian and female identity, have a deep and inseparable bond. Canada is oppressed by the presence of "Big Brother" America and finds it extremely difficult to live independently. America, on the contrary, is not only apathetic to the existence of its weaker neighbor, it exerts a negative influence through popular means of communication like the cable network, and the radio. Even though one may not call it physical congress, direct invasion, or propaganda, it is a subtle infiltration of another's space, attacking the minds of a people through media which fascinates the masses. Had it been a mutual exchange of influences, it would be perfectly healthy and desirable. The problem lies in it being a one-way affair, the stronger power exerting its influence—often baneful—over the weaker. Consequently, the weaker nation cannot grow normally and remains stunted. "The whole area of communication," says Atwood, "is something we pay a lot of attention to, and it is pretty much a one-way mirror. We can see everything you do, and you can't see a thing we do" [Interview 229].

In her essay, "Canadian-American Relations," she again explains how Canadians have remained obsessed with the U.S. to such an extent that they have forgotten their own culture and traditions: "They'd forgotten. They had their ears pressed to the wall for so long, listening in on the neighbors, who *were* rather loud, that they'd forgotten how to speak and what to say. They'd become addicted to the one-way mirror of the Canadian-American border—we can see you, you can't see us—and had neglected that other mirror, their own culture" [*Second Words* 385]. The conflict remains clearly defined in Atwood's works, the political tensions becoming allegories for other conflicts. As Jane Schhieter says, Canada and America are not actual countries but states of mind [Spanckeren xxii]. The two are distinct from each other, each viewing the other with suspicion because of their mutual differences. Whereas the stronger nation appears sinister in the eyes of the weaker, the latter in comparison, is perhaps a despicable weakling to be treated with contempt. While one is the big bad wolf, the other the helpless victim. The pattern is fixed, whether the two parties in question are countries or individuals. But, how does one cope with this given situation? Given the circumstances, how does one survive? Given a fixed geographical locale, how would a country survive in the oppressive presence of a bullying nation? Again, given fixed socio-cultural contexts, how would women hold their own? How would one continue to exist with dignity and respect despite predetermined negative patterns? This is what Atwood's writings are all about.

Nationalism and gender, thus, are closely linked. In both the question is that of power and subjugation. Nationalism, says Atwood, is "only defined as a problem by imperialist countries, for whom it is a problem because it means the colonies are acting up. For the colonies it's not nationalism that's the problem. It's imperialism. It's like the woman problem. Well, women are a problem for men, when they start acting up" [*Ibid.* 223]. In Atwood's *Power Politics*, the main issue is sexual politics. Each poem in the collection speaks of man-woman relations. But these relations are linked with a wider politics involving enemy countries. The poems are spoken in the first person, a female voice addressing a male "you." Thus they have the immediacy that comes with such narration, an "I" speaking to a "you." And yet, sadly, the intimacy between the speaker and the addressee is deceptive, for there is nothing but resentment and hostility between them. One is the aggressor, the other the victim:

...you cover me

with flags, a dark red
season, you delete from me
all other colours. [p. 41]

The imagery used for describing the relationship is imperialist in nature: one is not sure whether Atwood is describing the psychological subjugation of a woman or the political conquest of a geographical space. In any case, there is little difference for the two are alike. The colonizer/colonized relationship may be found between two nations or two individuals. A conquered nation suffers just the way an oppressed woman does, an idea that is made explicit in the poem entitled "They are hostile nations" [p. 37]. The subject is the senseless animosity between the sexes. Voicing a sentiment close to Matthew Arnold in "Dover Beach," Atwood says that in this chaotic, polluted world where everything seems to be heading for extinction, there should be love and understanding between the sexes. "Instead we are opposite, we / touch as though attacking." It does not seem to make sense. Why should there not be an effort towards harmony, for

We need each others'
breathing warmth, surviving
is the only war
we can afford.... [p. 38]

Instead of a mutual co-existence, there is hostility; instead of understanding and sympathy there is distrust. Love, which must have existed at some stage, has been distorted and ossified into resentment bordering on hatred.

In international politics the warring factions are hostile nations but in gender politics it is the male world versus the female. The two parties are contrasted at great length in *Power Politics*. From the very first page, the "you" is given parasitic connotations:

You fit into me
like a hook into an eye

a fish hook
an open eye

The differences between the two may be noted: the eye is "open" and so vulnerable while the hook forcibly intrudes, penetrates, hurts, and destroys. The one is weak, the other ruthless. The "eye" is what looks around and sees, is aware of the world outside its own existence. At the same time, it is a play on the "I," the individual aspects of the person, implying that the female speaker of the poem is capable of going into the depths of her inner self and understanding her desires and aspirations. The man's world is a closed one, a world that begins and ends with himself, where everything exists in relation to him alone. This is the basic difference between the two which is responsible for all other differences.

The picture on the title page of the book, which shows two figures, one presumably male and the other female, illustrates the differences between the two sexes. The female figure is suspended upside down by the left foot, tied up in what look like bandages. The other is an upright figure, completely covered in a suit of armor and holds a sword. Despite her trussed state, the woman's limbs show signs of flexibility which may be contrasted with the rigid posture of the other figure. Her eyes are wide open and seem unafraid. In fact, in every manner, she may be contrasted with the man in the armor. And yet they are bound together, for his right hand is tied up with her left foot. The picture becomes a comment on the title of the book and illustrates the main theme of the poems: although men and women are opposed to each other, they are inextricably bound and must co-exist. They need each other for self-definition. There is a poem [on p. 7], partly descriptive of the cover illustration, which begins thus:

My beautiful wooden leader
with your heartful of medals
made of wood, fixing it
each time so you almost win....

... General, you enlist
my body in your heroic
struggle to become real....

The poem places the man on horseback, riding roughshod over all his victims. As an equestrian "General," he is such a great hero on the battlefield that he mistakes personal relationships also to be fields for conquest. He is obviously manipulative, "fixing it" so that he almost wins every time. And yet victory, to be meaningful, must be asserted over something or someone. Every oppressor needs a victim. This is where the female speaker comes into the picture. This is where she is indispensable. The General needs horses. He needs armies to command. He needs prisoners. Without them he and his glory would have no meaning.

There is in the speaker's voice a note of contempt for the General. He may be adorned with medals and other paraphernalia of military glory, but he is "wooden," not human. His glory is illusory: a few medals pinned on to the chest are no proof of his power, nor are the hordes of terrified female followers whom he coerces into paying tributes. He may delude himself with false notions of his glory, but the fact remains that he is neither respected nor obeyed.

Magnificent on your wooden horse
you point with your fringed hand;
the sun sets, and the people all
ride off in the other direction.

Moreover, the suit of armor that he wears prevents him from moving freely, so he remains trapped in his outfit. This is ironical as his aim is actually to trap and bind others. The heady feeling of power so intoxicates him that he finds himself frozen in circumstances of his own creation, caught in a warlike bind that he can neither cope with nor break out of. He is incapable of leading his army. Who is, then, to be pitied more? The woman speaker who is aware of the situation and can analyze and comment on it? Or the power-blind "General" unable to look beyond the armor that encases and paralyzes him? The poem describes the woman as paralyzed, and with blinded eyes. In reality, it is the man who is paralyzed and who is metaphorically blinded although he may not be aware of it.

The poem that follows begins with related images: "Like eggs and snails you have a shell" [p. 8]. What, one may ask, is the shell for? Is it for protection or self-defense? Does the man feel threatened? Or does he suffer from insecurity? It seems ridiculous that he should feel threatened when it is he himself who is an unhealthy influence and a danger to all forms of life: "You move / from place to place like a disease // Like mushrooms you live in closets / and come out only at night." There is a sense of evil present in this description. It is like the serpent in the Garden of Eden creeping in to inject poison in Eve's perfect universe. The secrecy, the claustrophobic, unhealthy, parasitic, closed nature of man's world is emphasized. And, it may be noted, he creeps into territory which is not rightfully his. In other words, he is trying to appropriate another's space. The reaction is not unexpected:

> Imperialist, keep off
> the trees I said.
>
> No use: you walk backwards,
> admiring your own footprints. [p. 15]

Imperialist versus the trees that will most likely be cut down. Trees would be representative of the territory to be conquered. The female gender depicted as trees would also point to the tenacity of women, their struggle to survive in the face of all hostility.

The narcissistic, self-admiring, self-congratulatory male attitude, "admiring [his] own footprints" may be contrasted with the speaker's namelessness:

> I can't tell you my name:
> you don't believe I have one.... [p. 54]

It is not that she wishes to remain anonymous; the plain and simple fact is that it does not matter to man whether or not she has a name. He is indifferent to all except that which concerns him. This self-centeredness makes his world a closed one. Repeatedly, Atwood associates the male world with a closed, claustrophobic circle. The female world, on the contrary, is one of vast open spaces, stretches of land visible to the eye from a distance. "Imperialist, keep off / the trees," says the poet, focusing on the contrast between ecology and all damaging, poisoning, polluting influences, an idea made more explicit elsewhere, where "He is like a strange biological phenomenon" [p. 8], like a leech or a parasite, destroying whatever comes its way. The picture that comes to mind is William Blake's "The Sick Rose," where the blown rose, a symbol of innocent sexuality, is destroyed by the parasitic worm. As in Blake's poem, in Atwood's cosmology a healthy female world is poisoned and destroyed by the baneful effects of male intrusion. This female world is "open" and, for this reason, vulnerable to attack. The male world, on the contrary, is like a closed fist, ready to strike and destroy: "Fists have many forms; / a fist knows what it can do" [p. 31]. The fist can become dangerous, too. It may take the form of a sinister, malignant, growth that kills slowly but surely:

> yes at first you
> go down smooth as
> pills, all of me
> breathes you in and then...
>
> ...I flake apart
> layer by
> layer down
> quietly to the bone, my skull
> unfolds to an astounded flower
>
> too much of
> this is fatal. [p. 22]

The point of contact between the two parties is invariably accompanied by violence of some kind; the outcome is never a happy one. It is either a physical violence when the stronger party destroys the weaker, or it is a psychological violence when the weaker party is brow-beaten into submission, silence, and powerlessness.

Repeatedly, what is emphasized is the sheer physical dominance of the male, whether he is a General, or just another pompous leader throwing his weight around like a megaphone

> You become slowly more public,
> in a year there will be nothing left
> of you but a megaphone.... [p. 30]

A megaphone blaring away orders to be followed blindly, or perhaps a "set of instructions" representing the patriarchal order. In this public role, all tenderness, all finer points of personal relationships are lost:

> ... your kiss no longer literature
> but fine print, a set of instructions.

"Fine print," difficult to read, even more difficult to follow. That is what the conqueror's language is all about. As a result, communication between the ruler and the ruled is impossible, the one incapable of communicating, the other not being allowed to:

> Why talk when you are
> helmeted with numbers
>
> Language, the fist
> proclaims by squeezing
> is for the weak only. [p. 31]

When one is a part of an army controlled by a ruthless power, there is no point, indeed, trying to reason through verbal language. There is a total lack of communication. Again, the closed nature of the male world and the openness, the willingness to communicate, of the female, is highlighted. As a later poem puts it, "there is something in your throat that wants / to get out and you won't let it" [p. 34]. "You," the general, the megaphone, or the "impervious glass tower" [p. 32], can only give impersonal orders, but cannot communicate or respond to deeper feelings.

The two worlds, male and female, are poles apart in every respect. Atwood's interest in polarities is obvious from the contrasting patterns of their behavior and characteristics. It is possible to highlight their differences so far enumerated in the following manner (the numbers indicate the text pages):

Male	Female
Public figure:	Private person:
general 7	regimented army 31
imperialist 15	struggling for survival 23
narcissistic 15	caring, outward person
megaphone 30	nameless 54
monster 49	hapless victim 3
demanding	giving
death image 53	nurturing role 43
Unable to communicate:	Need for communication:
closed 34	open world 1
use of force as language 31	gift of words
silence 44	need to communicate 44
Selfish love:	Unselfish love:
mirror image	Giving and caring
unchanging	metamorphosis 4
Rock-like 36	like water 41
mobility, lack of fixity 54	tree-like, fixed, rooted 15

(The last two attributes, fixity and mobility, may seem to contradict the nature of love but, it may be noted, the negative aspects of both are associated with man while the positive with woman.) Such a list may appear to be biased and one-sided, but Atwood takes care to give illustrations each time. So the poems of *Power Politics* turn out to be a collection of vignettes, scenes and episodes taken at different times and places. The common theme remains that of power politics between the sexes.

In her *Selected Poems*, as David Buchbinder points out, Atwood uses the Homeric model to depict three different types of women: the victim (Circe), victimizer (Siren), and victor (Penelope), and it is this metaphor, running through the poems, that makes *Selected Poems* a unified text [Buchbinder 122-141]. Atwood focuses on the "ambiguity in the Homeric model of female figures who are simultaneously subordinate to male ones, yet powerful" [*Ibid.* 124]. Even though the poems of *Power Politics* do not present these Homeric female figures, they do center on the ambiguity associated with women: their helplessness along with their power. Circe or the Sirens may be clever enough to entice travelers, but the former is ultimately abandoned by Odysseus while the trio remain trapped in a role they cannot escape from. Similarly, Penelope may be the final victor, winning back her man, but she was the one who was abandoned initially. Thus, although they are strong, yet these women are weak. In the *Power Politics* poems there is the Penelope motif [p. 28] of a woman waiting for a departed lover. The other women who figure have the same ambiguous Homeric characteristics: they are weak yet strong. If man is depicted as a cannibalistic monster, woman is not one who may be "eaten" (Atwood's metaphor of the "edible" woman) easily for she fights back. "This above all, to refuse to be a victim," says the last chapter of *Surfacing*, is woman's duty to herself, an idea amply illustrated in *Power Politics*, at times through the imperialist analogy, and at times with reference to the ecology of the world which has female connotations, is life-giving but remains threatened by life-denying male forces.

While creating temporal frames for her poems, Atwood tries to connect the past with the present. Doing so, she toys with the concept of history. What is the use of history? Why is it important? And important, no doubt, it is! Lacking a history, one would have to invent one:

> Because we have no history
> I construct one for you [p. 26]

A relationship that lacks a history would be one that is formed in the immediate present, a relationship unburdened by the past. It could also be a relationship in which one (the male partner) has not been able to communicate the past clearly, and therefore the need to invent one. The woman's construction of history is an attempt to understand, to communicate, to fill up the gaps in their relationship. It also throws a light on the complexities of their relationship. On the one hand is his reticence, his unwillingness to communicate his personal history; on the other, her desire to know him and his background better—"Why should I need to explain you"—shows some kind of an obsession with him. She is totally involved with him:

> I invent, now and then
> an object, a watch, a picture
> you claim as yours.... [*ibid.*]

He looms like a huge monster (or superman, perhaps) on her mindscape. For her there seems to be no escape. And yet, she is aware that man is nothing but a myth created by woman. It is she who is responsible for all his destructive propensities. This is another way of saying that man is not born a man but made one—by woman:

> It was my fault but you helped,
> you enjoyed it. [p. 55]

There are regrets: "How can I stop you // Why did I create you [?]" she asks [p. 47]. But perhaps it is not too late to undo the wrong. At least an awareness has dawned that a mistake has been made, that a myth which should have been nipped in the bud has been created and nourished.

Why did woman create the myth of the superman? Perhaps to fulfill some foolish romantic dream: some dream inspired by an idyllic scene showing Adam and Eve in the garden of Eden:

> flakes of snow fall endlessly
> over an ornamental scene,
> a man and woman, hands joined and running....

Such was the dream. Such were the reasons why woman invented the myth of man and gave him a history, a place in a temporal frame. The results were ironical, certainly not what she wanted: for man, like Frankenstein's monster, turned upon his creator, bringing death and destruction:

> Nothing I can do will slow you
> down...
>
> You are serious, a gift-bearer,
> you set one foot
> in front of the other
>
> through the weeks and months, across
> the rocks, up from
> the pits and starless
> deep nights of the sea
>
> towards firm ground and safety. [p. 56]

As a contrast to the vision of Adrienne Rich, Atwood does not dream of a woman's utopia. She does not imagine a world without men. For her both male and female must co-exist although they are opposed to each other. Atwood's work is concerned with polarities, contraries, and antitheses. This is amply illustrated in her work where repeated images of dual-edgedness may be found. Take, for instance, her. "Two-headed Poems," or "The Double Voice," or *Double Persephone*. Life without dualities is unthinkable for Atwood, whether she speaks of power politics at the personal level or at a wider, global level: colonization, victimization, vulnerability of both women and land—"They're all paradigms of dominance / subservience," she says.

It is possible to conclude with Atwood's belief that "there are no stories I can tell my friends / that will make them feel better." Dissatisfied with stories, she looks for the truth, convinced that nothing else will work, nothing else will do justice to the present situation:

> If we make stories for each other
> about what is in the room
> We will never have to go in.
>
> ["Hesitations Outside the Door"]

Two options are presented: one, to live in an ostrich-like world of make-belief and, two, walking into the room to face reality. While the first would be a very comfortable, convenient approach, the second could disturb us out of our complacencies and compel us to revise our beliefs and attitudes. In gender relationships it may be far easier to carry on making up stories and shutting all doors to reality. But such an attitude is no longer possible. Doors have to be opened, reality has to be examined, and the truth has to be told. And the truth that women wish to see is not that which the patriarchal world sees but as it appears in its totality, the whole truth, complete and uncompromised. In such a totality, women will appear neither as angels nor as whores but as the human creatures they are:

> ...if you are not an angel, if you happen to have human failings, as most of us do, especially if you display any kind of strength or power, creative or otherwise, then you are not human. You are worse than human, you are a witch, a Me-

dusa, a destructive, powerful, scary monster.

[Margaret Atwood in "The Curse of Eve or [What I Have Learned at School," 25]

Bringing the witch, the Medusa, the monster back from the margin to the center is what Atwood's writings are committed to.

Rejecting the Father: Stevie Smith

There's a stake in your fat black heart
And the villagers never liked you.
They are dancing and stamping on you.
They always *knew* it was you.
Daddy, daddy, you bastard, I'm through.

Sylvia Plath, "Daddy"

Stevie Smith (1902-1971) was not consciously a feminist. She did not make any statements supporting the social or political rights of women. She did not participate in any organized rallies for the improvement of women's lot. Nor did she adopt radical postures in her personal behavior or appearance or lifestyle. In fact she lived the life of a drudge, at work slaving away at a desk job almost all her life, and at home devoting her energies to caring for her family, rummaging bargain stores and flea markets in search of a good bargain, trying to making both ends meet on a shoe-string budget. No, nothing about Stevie Smith, neither her appearance nor her style of living, nothing was unconventional or bohemian. And yet, smoldering beneath the conventional, mousy appearance was a rebellious spirit which questioned all the norms that women were expected to follow, the age-old beliefs that tradition had handed down, the coercive authority of patriarchy that suppressed all signs of enterprise or individuality in women.

When Stevie Smith first started writing, the women's movement was, so to speak, in the doldrums. It was a time of transition, a period of uncertainty that lay between the first signs of restlessness among women and the gradual dawn of realization that something should be done to improve their lot in society. There was the beginning of awareness of the injustices and the economic and legal inequalities suffered by women, but the protest was neither intelligently organized nor even fully articulated. There was no consolidated body to champion women's cause, no role models to emulate, no women patrons to turn to. In such a situation, a woman could only depend on herself and her own resources. Stevie knew she was alone in her dissatisfaction, just as thousands of women like her were alone. Aware that she had to first strengthen herself for the task, she steeled herself, willing herself to be strong, keeping all emotional baggage at arm's length, and constantly reminding herself of the various ways in which women could be exploited by the opposite sex, and particularly of how she personally had suffered because of a wayward and irresponsible father. In fact, this is what molds much of Stevie Smith's poetry. She never let herself forget the injustice her father meted out to her sister, her mother and herself. Her life was one long and brave struggle against humdrumness, against mediocrity and depression caused by countless privations at home and a lackluster secretarial job in the office.

Stevie Smith's father had a wandering, restless spirit that yearned to roam freely through the world. His ambition to join the Navy was thwarted by a possessive mother so, much against his will, he joined the family coal business. The lure of the wide world, the rolling ocean and the blue skies, however, was not to be denied. When his business started declining, he finally left for the sea, leaving behind his wife and two daughters, aged five and three years, to fend for themselves. Stevie Smith never forgave this great betrayal. She and her sister were brought up amid great hardship and penury by their mother and their aunt, immortalized by Stevie later in her prose work as "The Lion of Hull." An autobiographical poem entitled "The House of Mercy," graphically describes the situation. Theirs was, as she puts it, a "house of female habitation" comprising two ladies, one of them "Mrs S." who was left with two baby girls by a husband who had absconded:

> He soon left them and went away to sea,
> Nor sent them money, nor came home again
> Except to borrow back

> Her Naval Officer's Wife's Allowance from Mrs S.
> Who gave it him at once, she thought she should.
> ["The House of Mercy"]

Her resentment, it may be noted, is directed not only against the father but also against the mother for allowing herself to be so exploited by her husband, for being a willing pawn in his treachery to the family. However, in spite of the absence of the male head of the family, or perhaps because of it, the household is remembered as one in which there was warmth and love, with all its female inhabitants totally devoted to loving and caring for one another. In fact the father's periodic returns to the fold, the intermittent reminders of his existence, are something of a nuisance as they simply drained further the family's meager resources.

This desertion by her father was the crucial episode in Stevie Smith's life which was to shape and color her thoughts throughout her life. It aroused in her, in the first place, a distrust of men, an anger against all those who shirked their responsibilities towards their dependents for the sake of their own selfish pursuits. This was accompanied by an equally vehement frustrated anger against women who connived with the men to let their gender be exploited: women who were either too weak or too short-sighted to realize that they were being taken advantage of. As an alternative to the weak, exploited woman, Stevie visualized a stronger woman, even one sinister and vengeful, capable of taking care of herself. The father's betrayal also led to a protest against all forms of authority, a questioning of conventional norms, a challenging of traditionally held beliefs in male superiority and patriarchal domination. Instead, Stevie Smith presents new perspective on old institutions and doctrines. She demythologizes accepted beliefs only to make her readers, particularly female readers, aware of the pitfalls their ignorance may lead them into. As Sanford Sternlicht puts it, she expresses the spirit of her times: "Stevie symbolized the pain, the passion, and the zaniness of the time, as well as the frustration, the melancholy, the bewilderment, the rage, and the incipient revenge of contemporary womanhood; for the very same forces, wrongs, and awakenings that caused the women's movement to come into being had created the impetus for the poetry of Stevie Smith" [Sternlicht 3].

What may be noted, however, is that although Stevie Smith had a lot to be discontented about, the anger and frustration she felt is kept well in control. Not for her the agitated ravings of a Sylvia Plath or a Diane Wakoski. She voices her protest against the patriarchal order in a very subtle, civilized manner. There is a genteel quality about Smith's poetry which speaks volumes for the culture she was groomed in, the culture she knew she had to conform to in order to survive in a world that was indifferent to women's aspirations. The restraint that she exercised in her poetry may, perhaps, give one the impression that it lacks in intensity. But this is not so. It is her intellectual grasp of the situation which is evident everywhere, which enabled her to see the funny side of a pathetic situation, which gave her the courage to bear sorrows in her personal and also professional life. So, intellectually treated, pain loses its barb and is objectified. Sufferings, when they are laughed at, become bearable—which certainly does not mean that they do not exist. Stevie Smith's poetry, thus, does not indulge in any kind of whining or moaning or self-pitying *angst*. It gives evidence of a mind that is always in control of itself and expresses its ideas subtly through humor and wit.

Take, for instance, a poem in which she mentions her personal animosity towards her father: "Papa Love Baby," which presents the viewpoint of a child. From her baby-carriage, her vision of the world is an unromantic, absurd one. In Smith's poetry generally the children are realistic and wise, while the grown-ups are foolish. worthy only of scorn. The poem mentions both the parents as rather absurd: the mother, in her folly, is romantic, while the father is the sort even a child would not respect:

> My mother was a romantic girl
> So she had to marry a man with his hair in curl
> Who subsequently became my unrespected papa
> But that was a long time ago now.

The last line quoted, "But that was a long time ago now," removes the entire story to such a distance that one may look at it objectively, and get the picture in its totality, without any excessive emotion or passion. Distanced thus in time, the child narrator can comprehend the folly of the entire situation, how it was a misalliance between her parents, a misalliance that occurred only because her mother nurtured some foolish romantic dreams in her heart. The poet's disappointment is directed at the mother for being naive to a fault, for being gullible enough to be taken in by a man whose only asset was a charming physical appearance. And yet, it had to happen: because, unfortunately, she was romantic, she was so fated to make a foolish marriage. It could not have been any other way. Stevie Smith does not show any preference for one parent over the other. Both deserve contempt because both are ridiculous. Perhaps her mother would have been more respectfully referred to had she held her own against the father. If she had shown some awareness of her mistake, or if she had somehow made amends for her mistake, her daughter would have remembered her more charitably. But, no, as "The House of Mercy" tells us, she allowed her husband to exploit her, letting him take away even the small allowance she received as a naval officer's wife.

This rejection of her parents, that is, the rejection of authority is part of Stevie Smith's rebellion against injustice. She takes an irreverent view of family relationships, questioning accepted notions of filial love:

> What folly it is that daughters are always supposed to be
> In love with papa.

Why should it be so? This is not the question she asks. Her question is—whoever said so? The objection to the idea is implicit. Unquestioning love for the parent, according to her, is absurd because the child's vision of the world, being far more accurate than that of the adults, enables her to see the absurdities of the grown-up world and the mistakes the adults make. With this clarity of vision it is unthinkable that she should nurture in her heart any illusions, any sentimental love or affection for she knows the price her mother has paid for being a sentimental, foolish girl. Stevie Smith closes her doors to the slightest suggestion of emotional weakness. In order to survive, she knows she has to be tough and unsentimental. Through all her poems she keeps sentiments at bay. This is the survival technique she adopts.

Instead of love, tenderness, and other emotions Stevie Smith's poetry upholds just the opposite. There is, in "Papa Love Baby," for instance, something close to hate with which the baby responds to her father's love: "I tried to hide it, but it showed in my eyes unfortunately." The question that may be asked is: why does the baby dislike the father so? Is it because of the way he has deceived her mother? Or because the deception may be directed at herself, too? Both, perhaps. Evidently, there is also gender politics involved in the antagonism as the male deceiver is trying to win over the opposite sex, that is, the mother and the child. The mother may have deliberately closed her eyes to the fact, but not the child. Implicit is a reversal of roles here, with the mother being depicted as ignorant and the child as the wise one who will stand no nonsense and who will certainly not be taken in by any sentimental humbug. The mother is rejected partly because she has been foolishly sentimental but mainly because she seems to reinforce patriarchal values here in the poem as elsewhere in Stevie Smith's work. The father is repudiated because he has tried to play a sentimental game with the child, a game which brought him success with the mother. His efforts at winning over the daughter fail miserably as the child turns away from him, convinced that she is better off on her own, without either of the foolish parents.

The same idea is repeated in "My Hat, " which is escapist in theme. A piece of wishful thinking, it fantasizes a parent-less world where one may live and grow freely, without any distorting influences on the individual's personality. And again, parents are rejected partly because they are foolish, and partly because they uphold an undesirable patriarchal system. The world of the parents is clearly inane and preposterous. As in "Papa Love Baby" the perspective presented is the child's. Stevie Smith again presents the child's vision and turns to the fairy-tale world. The child is older now, ready for marriage in fact, but her vision of the world is as clear and uncluttered as before, without any adult-inspired false notions. Moreover, she retains her interest in fairy tales remembered from childhood. Just as fairy-tales present characters flying through the air on broomsticks or other magic agents, Smith in her poem is transported to a dream world by means of a magic hat which, ironically, was given to her by her mother:

> Mother said if I wore this hat
> I should be certain to get off with the right sort of chap
> Well look where I am now, on a desert island....

This is not what the mother had in mind, but it has somehow turned to the daughter's advantage. The mother's desire was that the daughter should look attractive enough to make a convenient, conventional marriage to a nice (albeit dull and uninteresting) young man, the "right sort of chap." This, according to the mother, conditioned by the patriarchal society, was the proper destiny of women.

The hat becomes symbolic of a conventional role that society requires the daughter to play: that of a beautiful, obedient wife. Carrying out the part successfully would win her social approval. And what then? The mother wanted her daughter to look attractive and, sure she looks attractive. But the mother was thinking only of the onlookers, the male-dominated world which had to pass judgment on whether or not the girl would make an attractive bride. What she overlooked was the fact that foisting a role on the girl could bring about a change in her personality. This is what happens: the plain, unattractive girl undergoes a heady transformation as she realizes the power of her physical beauty. Like the ugly duckling, she turns into a swan:

> What a moment that was as I rose up, I rose like a flying swan
> As strong as a swan too....

The image of the swan here signifies the birth of a new personality, the blossoming of a flower that was not allowed to bloom hitherto. This is implicit in the use of the "rose" in the lines which, although a verb, could easily stand for a noun, the blooming flower in all its glory. Just as the swan needs no props once it is aware of its beauty so, too, the daughter, once she is confident of her power and her glory ("Ah, I thought, How this hat becomes me."), she abandons all fettering ties and relationships, all constricting bonds, soaring away into uncharted skies. The fairy-tale/nursery-rhyme technique is not abandoned. There is a sense of wide-eyed wonder at the glorious flight through a magic space "Between the sun and the moon," and at the world she has been carried to, where

> It is always morning here on this peculiar island
> The grass grows into the sea on the dipping land....

Peculiar? Indeed, that is how it would be viewed by the world she has left behind. But as for the girl, this is the world of her dreams, a world in which she would gladly stay on:

> Am I glad I am here? Yes, well, I am,
> It's nice to be rid of Father, Mother and the young man....

A utopia, it gives her the much desired liberation from the shackles of conventional, claustrophobic living.

There is something curiously Blakean in the childlike tone that Stevie Smith adopts in her poems. Accompanied as they are by ingenuous sketches, or "doodles" as she called them, the poems read like songs of innocence before the shades of experience set in. They have a spontaneity, a candidness which places them on a plane different from that by other women writers. Smith is also Blakean in her rejection of authority. She seems to agree with William Blake that the church, the parent, and the teacher are all evil institutions bent on distorting one's personality, crushing the individual growth of a person. Blake's categories of malevolent influences, are rolled into one comprehensive figure by Smith—that representing male authority, whether it is the father, or a suitor, or even a mother who has internalized male values. This is evident in a poem like "My Hat."

Elsewhere, she directs her gaze at religion. What is religion but the favorite occupation of those who have little to do. Take Mrs Simpkins, for example:

> Mrs Simpkins never had very much to do
> So it occurred to her one day that the Trinity wasn't true....
> ["Mrs Simpkins"]

Now, if she were neck-deep in work, with no time to spare, would her thoughts idly turn to religion? This is the irreverent question nagging at Smith's mind. What is God and who is he, if not a man-made construct, a convenient peg on which one may anchor one's thoughts? If one pauses to analyze what goes into the making of the concept of Christ there are many loop-holes which are hard to explain away. This is what Stevie Smith tries to highlight in her poem "Was He Married?" which raises objections with childlike innocence. But the innocent tone carries the weight of wisdom and the child's questions are eye-openers, just as though she were protesting, "But the Emperor is wearing no clothes!" Again, using the child's clarity of vision, Smith poses very valid questions that undermine the logic behind our religious beliefs and challenge the validity of the assumptions handed down to us.

"Was He Married?" is in the form of a dialogue between a mother and her daughter. It is interesting to note that the sketch accompanying the poem shows the daughter in a chair and the mother incongruously seated at her feet. This is not simply an eccentricity or whim on the poet's part: there is a logic underlying the illustration which connects the poem with other poems like "Papa Love Baby" and "My Hat." This is, as the poet calls it, an "argument poem" [Sternlicht 31]. It tries to demythologize Christ through a volley of questions that undermine the very basis of Christianity. The main idea it questions is whether one may consider Christ to be human if He never experienced any human suffering, pain, anger, grief, or remorse. The young inquirer of the poem questions Christ's participation in the human experience while the other (the adult voice of the mother) simply reiterates His divinity, repeating time-worn clichés propagated by Christianity. The child focuses on the shortcomings and handicaps of Christ, an idea that the religious-minded would, perhaps, consider blasphemous. In a persistent, nagging tone, the child applies the human yardstick to Jesus Christ. Her questions vary in range from the personal to the social and political, beginning with the absurd idea of Christ's marital status:

> Was he married, did he try
> To support as he grew less fond of them
> Wife and family?

To which the mother answers in the negative, that He "never suffered such a blow," a telling statement which contrasts man's fate with Christ's. Unlike Christ, man is not spared the so-called misfortune of falling out of love with a wife and family that hangs like a millstone around his neck, a family that he is duty-bound to support, or else face social censure. This idea seems to divide the family into two parties: the husband on the one side, and the wife and children on the other. The husband may change his mind, growing "less fond of" his dependents, but does the other party comprising the wife and the children, have this option? The answer is understood: no. No, the wife and the children are too dependent on the husband to even think of an alternative to the situation. So, not only is the husband's action tolerated, it is even condoned. The unfortunate man suffers a "blow," as his wife sympathetically puts it: an idea which the child finds hard to accept.

It is significant that while the mother remains more or less unaware of the absurdities of the system she lives within, the child is the one who, in the process of sorting out things for herself, forces this realization on her. With the dawning of wisdom, the child grows up, out of innocence and into experience. "Was He Married?", thus, traces a rite of passage, showing the evolution of the child's convictions, shifting from the religious dogmas handed down by authority, to a logical analysis and repudiation of those dogmas in favor of more rational, albeit unconventional, beliefs. Trying her hardest to identify Christ with a human being, the child shifts her attention from the social concept of matrimony to emotional states. Did the Son of Man ever feel weak, neglected, or lonely? Did he ever have any feelings of inadequacy? Did he experience fluctuations of moods, from deep depression to a soaring euphoria? The mother's answer being again in the negative, the child comes to the logical conclusion that because human beings suffer, and because god does not, it is human beings who are more worthy of admiration:

> All human beings should have a medal,
> A god cannot carry it, he is not able.

The questions that the child asks are relevant to what she has observed in the world around her. Human beings suffer various psychological and emotional sorrows, social and political problems. They face adversity stoically and they look up to Christ with awe and reverence. Why? Looking at the logistics of Christology, the child can find no valid reason why man should worship someone supposedly created in his own likeness but, in reality, so different from him that He has never shared any of his experience of anguish or sorrow.

A theological debate, the poem tries to figure out whether Christ is human or divine. Clearly, the child is convinced that He cannot be human because He has not suffered pain and sorrow. Well, He must be a god, then. And what exactly is a god? Cornered by the child's nagging questions, the mother is forced to admit that

> A god is Man's doll, you ass,
> He makes him up like this on purpose.
>
> He might have made him up worse.

"He might have made him up worse"—this statement by the mother shows that all along she was aware of something not very right about the way gods are worshipped. And yet, she had avoided confronting the issue because challenging accepted notions would, perhaps, lead to an open conflict and cause more problems. God is "Man's doll"—the capital "M" that Smith uses could possibly point to the male section of mankind which tends to impose its ideology on women who do not oppose them and children who are too innocent to see through the politics behind the doctrines handed down to them. It may be noted that while it is Man with a capital M, the "god" remains uncapitalized. This would, then, imply that god is a figment of man's imagination, and what man tends to worship is an idealized image of himself. The legend of Christ, thus, may be interpreted as a wish-fulfilling male fantasy, a rather unusual idea but one that holds ground. Unfortunately, however, women have accepted the notion of Christ's superiority without questioning the rationale behind it.

This raises a very pertinent question: is the poem about Christ? Is it about god? Or is it about man (meaning the male of the species)? Perhaps it *is* about Jesus Christ whom Christianity sometimes calls divine and sometimes human, the product of a union between the Virgin Mary, who was a human being, and the Holy Spirit of god. In a sidelong manner, the poem refers to the concept of god: how man has created his deity in his own image. It may also be argued that Stevie Smith is speaking of men, and men alone, and the subtle ways in which they exert their superiority on women. This point of view may not strike the casual reader but a careful reading of the poem, keeping in mind the fact that it shows us two female speakers talking about a supposedly superior being, and keeping in mind the gender of that superior being and the tone of awe and reverence that is being used throughout, it would not be far-fetched to say that Stevie Smith is indirectly taking up cudgels on behalf of women, exposing the biased, sexist nature of most religious beliefs. When she voices the popularly held belief of God's superiority above all men—

> He was not inferior,

He was superior—

she is obliquely referring to the idea of male superiority which is generally imposed on women. Just as god is far above the trivial joys and sorrows that plague humanity, far above petty human politics, so is man considered a magnanimous creature, on an elevated plane that transcends all that is banal and female. To a large extent, because they do not question the idea of male superiority, women are to be blamed for letting them get away with exaggerated notions of their greatness: just as "god is Man's doll," deliberately created in such a form, so is man's power the outcome of women's reluctance to challenge authority that has been imposed on them.

The underlying idea seems to be one related to identification: on the one hand identifying a concept (that of god) and, on the other, identifying oneself with that concept. Can one possibly believe in a concept without identifying oneself with it somehow? Without feeling a bonding with it? Without the object of one's belief, in some way or the other, represents one's deepest hopes and aspirations? This is a point emphasized over and over again in the questions asked by the child. How can one possibly have faith in someone dissimilar to oneself? Were it a more "human" god or, in other words, were it a deity who lived and suffered the way human beings do, who felt the same pain and anguish, then the matter would not be so complicated. But the way things stand, when the concept of god is one that bears no kinship whatsoever with human experience, why should one have blind faith in it? This is the question reiterated in Stevie Smith's poem. And, no matter how biased one may be, one cannot deny that she has a valid point. Presented as an argument, logical and coherent, it appeals to the intellect and is hard to refute.

On a first reading of Stevie Smith's collected poems, it may be noted that what immediately strikes the reader is not her defiance or rejection of authority or even her resentment of an androcentric universe. What stands out most is, perhaps, her focus on death. Time and again her poems express a negation of life, a yearning for the oblivion of death. This could be taken as an escapist's turning away from the pressures of life, choosing death as a release from the agony of existence. This is one alternative to life explored by Stevie Smith. There are other alternatives, too. The manner in which she sometimes moves her attention away from men to focus on the world of nature may, again, be called escapist. Nature, clearly, is something man is not in tune with. Sometimes here, too, although male power is not obtrusively displayed, there is subtle evidence of it. For instance, by some kind of osmosis, man contaminates an otherwise perfect world with his negative characteristics:

> Nature has taught her creatures to hate
> Man that fusses and fumes
> Unquiet man
> As the sap rises in the trees
> As the sap paints the trees a violent green
> So rises the wrath of Nature's creatures
> At man.... ["Alone in the Woods"]

Nature is life-giving, but man's tendency to negate all that promotes a healthy and clean living injects poison into it. Nature is female and her world is violated by male insensitivity. When Stevie Smith turns to nature, or to the creatures of nature, she is in a way snubbing the patriarchal world, stating her preference for a life devoid of any human attachments or encumbrances, a world free of human (especially male) encroachments.

It is possible to conclude by saying that, broadly speaking, Smith's concern is the rejection of authority in all its tyrannical forms: the authority of an oppressive social system, the authority of a religion indifferent to the aspiration of human beings, or that of an unjust domestic tradition that refuses to change with the times. In particular, Smith is concerned with the repudiation of whatever systems inflict sufferings on women. Take, for instance, the scenes enacted within the house. In a poem like "The Queen and the Young Princess," Stevie Smith expresses her anger against domestic drudgery. Like "Was He Married?" the poem is in the form of a dialogue between a mother and her daughter. This time it questions not religious beliefs but social conventions that are unquestioningly accepted, the manner in which a woman is reduced to a drudge in a domestic situation. The child questions the mother on what lies ahead of her: "But what is my life that is to come to be?" And the mother replies: "Much the same, child, as it has been for me." Then comes a description of the mother's life:

> But Mother you often say you have a headache
> Because of the crown you wear for duty's sake.
> So it is, so it is, a headache I have
> And that is what you must grow up to carry to the grave.
> ["The Queen and the Young Princess"]

And what, one may wonder, is Stevie Smith's alternative to the household drudge? She would prefer a strong woman who can see through all the shams of social mores and how they operate only to subjugate the female sex, making women inferior, no matter what role they adopt in life.

In *Novel on Yellow Paper*, Stevie Smith marks the end of one kind of woman—the submissive, obedient kind—and the birth of another, more shrewd woman, who is aware of the games society plays and the role women are expected to adopt in the world of men:

> And so thinking how everything is all right because she is married, and how she must not be anything but very gentle and kind to the poor friend who is still not having any man to wash up for, but is still awfully inferior and unmarried, she must be very tactful and kind to this friend, and not, oh no, she must not say one word to make worse for this friend the awful burden of inferiority, how her arms are empty, and she has no *kiddy*.... [153-54]

A woman may still be "complete" even if she is not cooking and washing for a man or playing nurse to his children. All it needs is a change of perspective.

Perhaps an interesting alternative to the drab housewife, muses Smith half-seriously, would be the rogue woman of "Lady Rogue Singleton" who dispenses with all men and opts for a life on her own terms. She chooses to live alone, saying:

> I could never make you happy darling,
> Or give you the baby you want,
> I would always very much rather, dear,
> Live in a tent. ["Lady 'Rogue' Singleton"]

The lady would much rather live away from all that is considered genteel or civilized, whether it is the institution of marriage or domesticity, or both. She would much rather reject such "civilized" life and live in the wilderness, even if it means being branded as a "rogue" in the eyes of the patriarchal world. In another poem entitled "The Wedding Photograph," the rejection of the male is more sinister with the woman hinting at murder:

> So smile Harry smile and I will smile too
> Thinking what is going to happen to you.

Are these women *femmes fatale*? They seem to be. Clearly they are resentful of having their identity appended to a male who is supposed to control them. Hence their anger. By portraying the angry woman Smith shows us the constructive use of anger. Her ideal woman is one who can experience a healthy anger at the limitations imposed on her, one who is aware of her own powers, beauty, charms, and also aware of man's inadequacy, that man is actually an object of ridicule: "Will Man ever face fact and feel flat?" asks Smith. Flatness, literally denoting the male condition, implies that something is missing. It points to a lack which men suffer from. Women, on the other hand, are literally not "flat." Being well-endowed (with curves, for instance) they are more capable, if only they would wake up to this fact. If only they would become aware of their own self-sufficiency, if only they realize that they do not need to identify themselves in relation to men, and that man-made phallocentric laws are nothing but redundant in a female utopia. Such is the woman Stevie Smith appreciates. In a characteristically tongue-in-the-cheek manner she tries to awaken in her female readers the need to grow out of the conventional mold and develop into individual personalities, each unique, each a person and not a stereotype.

The Many Faces of Desire: Kamala Das

I have stretched my two dimensional
Nudity on sheets of weeklies, monthlies
Quarterlies, a sad sacrifice. I've put
My private voice away, adopted the
Typewriter's click as my only speech.

Kamala Das, "Loud Posters"

Kamala Das has always been a controversial poet. She has drawn critical attention not so much for the intrinsic merit of her poetry but for her uninhibited portrayal of female sexuality. Her professed autobiography, *My Story*, scandalized the complacent South-Indian Nair community to which she belongs and sent shock waves throughout the by-and-large conservative country. This essay on Kamala Das would first focus on the socio-cultural milieu that the poet began writing in, the influences that shaped her psyche, and the peculiar stimuli her creative impulse received from the external world. Then it would critically examine her poetry, focusing on the manner in which she portrays female desire and its ambivalence: on the fact that it is pulled in two contradictory directions, the one leaning towards traditionally imbibed beliefs, values, and principles, while the other pointing to a new stance which, although rooted in a phallocratic society, is unmistakably feminist and advocates the empowerment of woman.

Kamala Das is different from the other poets considered so far in that she belongs to a non-western milieu and is conditioned by social and cultural factors that in no way apply to the others. She writes as an Indian woman, steeped in the cultural ethos of a particular time, place, and people. It is in this chronotopic context that her poetry is to be understood. This does not, however, mean that her achievement is not comparable to that of her counterparts from the western world. On the contrary, there are numerous parallels and similarities in their thoughts. Like the Anglo-American feminists, she calls for a total re-thinking, a revisioning of a world, envisaging a new order where woman will receive her due dignity and respect. Like the French feminists, she focuses on her body, visualizing its needs and desires as a special language, a medium which a woman may use to communicate her deepest thoughts, her innermost feelings. Kamala Das is neither self-conscious nor apologetic about being a woman. For this reason, perhaps, she has been accused of brazenness. She has been at the receiving end of unjust criticism which stems mainly from critics who are groomed in a masculine tradition and choose to read her poems from a primarily male point of view.

In order to arrive at an understanding of the world in which Kamala Das's poems live and breathe, it is essential to turn to *My Story*, her controversial quasi-autobiographical narrative that incensed many of her critics. When a critic sees her story as "an experiment with sex under the pretext of a liberated woman, or an example of "pathetic exhibitionism and subtle eroticism" [Subba Rao] he is voicing the opinion critics generally have of her work, particularly male critics who look for and fail to find traditionally "feminine" qualities in a woman's work. What they fail to see is the reason behind these uninhibited expressions of desire. Why does Kamala Das feel the need to jolt the society with her blatant poems on sexual desire? Why does she feel she must flaunt her sexuality. The answers lie not in the narcissism of Kamala Das or on her allegedly limitless libido, but in the milieu that gives birth to such literature. Something somewhere in the society is responsible for the kind of poems Das writes. Were it a more liberal, permissive society, there would be no need to rudely awaken it. But having, as it did, a double set of values for its men and women, someone like Kamala Das was bound to rebel sooner or later. Whether the rebellion succeeds or fizzles out is another matter altogether.

The point around which much of the criticism revolves, whether or not *My Story* is a factual account of Das's life, is not relevant to the discussion here. It does not matter whether Kamala Das is writing about herself or about another woman, whether she is talking about her own experiences or someone else's, or whether the experiences relate to marital or extra-marital affairs. What matters is that she writes about female experience in a given set of circumstances. That she chooses to write in the first person and not through a surrogate, camouflaged third-person identity is a different point altogether, although it does point to her unconventional daring, her courage in the face of all the hostility she surely must have anticipated from old-fashioned orthodoxy. In *My Story*, Kamala Das portrays not simply a female character but also the society which nurtures her. So it is not just the story of a single individual but that of many institutions, traditions, persons, events and experiences (on a collective rather than individual level) that comprise the world of the central character of her narrative. Born and brought up in a traditional Nair family of Kerala, Das writes about a world that she is familiar with. She writes about its customs, manners, rituals, and traditions. In this society she has the role of an inside-outsider, in the sense that she belongs to it and is sufficiently familiar with its ways but, at the same time, she has traveled outside this small world and had enough exposure to other socio-cultural systems to be aware of the unsavory points of her own milieu and distinguish the positive aspects from the negative.

It may be noted that just by expressing her thoughts, Kamala Das is actually attacking the mores of a society that believes in the silence of women. She is indulging in an act that her community frowns upon. And when she speaks about sex and sexual experience, and especially when she recounts her personal sexual experiences, she is deliberately inviting the wrath of a shocked community. "I needed to disturb society out of its complacence. I found the complacence a very ugly state.... I wanted to remove the gender-difference," she says [Interviewed by Iqbal Kaur in *Perspectives on Kamala Das's Poetry* 167]. Aware of the bias that her society had against women who write, for a long time in the poems she published, she tried to hide under the androgynous name of K. Das which would successfully camouflage her gender.

My Story focuses on the double standards of social morality, on power-politics and power-imbalance in sexual relationships, and on a number of related social issues. It attempts to highlight the problems women face in a sexist culture, the hurdles that one has to encounter time and again if one wishes to change the laws of a male-oriented society. In a man's world a woman is little more than an object that plays a marginalized role. Her importance is assessed in relation to her family—her husband and children. Her existence as an individual is of little significance. Simone de Beauvoir's saying that "One is not born, but rather becomes a woman" was never more true of a poet other than Kamala Das.

Kamala Das's narrative begins with a mention of the dawn of the early consciousness of her political have-nots, the awareness that she belonged to an oppressed race. As a "little child growing up in Calcutta" (1) she was made aware that her brown skin was a disadvantage to her in a country which was ruled by the white man. She speaks about "the tortures we underwent at school for wearing under the school uniform of white twill a nut-brown skin." (2) On one occasion her brother, who was intellectually far ahead of his class, was deliberately hurt in the nose and made to bleed by a white class-mate who exclaimed in surprise, "Blackie, your blood is red." (2) Her brother did not retaliate, but the incident enraged Kamala who attacked the bully violently. Thus, from her childhood, Kamala Das displayed a strong refusal to accept injustice or unfairness. Her spirit rebelled against the racial oppression that she, with her people, had to suffer in her own country. Yet, sometimes there were moments when she wistfully imagined how wonderful it would be to belong to the privileged white class: "I wondered why I was born to Indian parents instead of to a white couple." (9) She would resent being part of a race which was colonized. Dark complexion was associated with inferiority while the white colonizers were regarded as a superior race. "Bearing the burden of a swarthy skin," Kamala Das entered adolescence in the pre-independence days, feeling helpless and frustrated, harboring a grudge against the British who still ruled the country and treated Indians like slaves. She could not accept servility. Nor could she accept the sycophantic behavior of those who tried to please the whites, "clowning to put them in good humor, barking like a dog and braying like an ass." (3)

Politically, no doubt, there was much to be wished for in the country. At the same time, there was oppression in the domestic and social spheres, too. In Das's family the system followed was matriarchy. Not that it differed much from patriarchy because, as Kate Millett argues [Millett 25], power-politics in matriarchy is not very much different from that of patriarchy. The difference lies in that male power is passed on to the next generation through a female descendant. In Kamala Das's family it meant that her maternal uncle was the head of the clan. Her mother was more or less indifferent to what went on around her, preferring to spend most of her time lying in bed writing poetry in Malayalam. Her father ruled supreme. Several times in her account of her childhood she refers to his autocratic ways and how he would lay down the rules of the household, insisting that they be followed. She remembers how he would "roar" and how rough his hands were as he forced Kamala and her brother to swallow castor oil. And if his children did not toe his line he had his own remedies:

> He had warned me that if I did not do well in Maths., he would marry me off. Unfortunately, I could never do well in Maths., and hence I was married off as a punishment. [Interview 161]

Marriage, thus, came to Das as a punishment for not coming up to male intellectual standards. Even later, when Kamala was unhappy as a married woman, her father thought he could set things right by re-orienting her towards a role that patriarchy inscribed for its women, and bought her a Singer sewing-machine (95). There were other elders in the family who demanded unquestioning obedience and respect: "It was not seemly for the child of an orthodox family to ask questions of importance and the elders expressed their resentment." (12) Her grandmother who was "orthodox and puritanical," represented the authoritarian yoke of tradition and convention which the family had to bear. Naturally, therefore, when the old woman died, for Kamala it was a "new-found freedom" (119).

The idea of remaining subservient to any form of authority irked the rebel in Kamala Das and she would miss no opportunity to defy it. Hers seems to be a defiant Blakean spirit that believes that as the caterpillar chooses the fairest leaves to lay its eggs on, so do social and religious dogmas lay their curse on the fairest of joys. The parent, the teacher, and the priest were all seen as autocratic figures bent on distorting the natural growth of an individual by enforcing the socially acceptable moral code. But is this moral code acceptable to the individual? Evidently, to Das it is not. Defiance of all forms of authority was natural for her. Right from her childhood she was drawn towards those who transgressed or deviated from convention. When she was advised not to associate with a girl of questionable character, she was "instantly drawn towards her" (81). She was infatuated with the charm of Govinda Kurup, "the outlaw" who had the guts to scrawl obscenities on the blackboard (21). When her teacher told her not to pay attention to a particular morally debauched man, she admits: "I felt I ought to meet him when I grew up, and perhaps become his mistress" (61). And at thirteen when she imagined herself in love with a student activist (64-65), what attracted her most to him was the fact that he was a non-conformist. Rather than meekly accept traditions and values handed down by society, Kamala Das, with a mind of her own and in conflict with inherited values, preferred to create her own terms, lay down her own laws.

The Nair household was a claustrophobic one where women and children remained stifled by age-old customs and conventions. The women, as the poet saw them, were naive to the point of being foolish. They were gullible, orthodox and superstitious. A scheming outsider would find it easy to take advantage of them, as when they were fooled by a mendicant who decided to live off them (67-68) despite the hostility of the menfolk of the house. These women were hypocritical and prudish in sexual matters. Sex, in the Nair community that Das grew up in, was an unmentionable topic: "the women of the best Nair families never mentioned sex" (26). There was nothing called sex-education. So most of the adolescent girls knew little or nothing about sex. To make matters worse, the tradition of child-marriage was prevalent. Marriages were arranged by the families when the girl was still a child. The groom chosen was much older, quite often a relative from the mother's side. The lack of sexual knowledge and the great age difference did not make adjustment an easy process. As she tells us: "It was customary for the Nair girl to marry when she was hardly out of her childhood and it was also customary for the much older husband to give her a rude shock by his sexual haste on the wedding night" (26). Das's own life was arranged with little regard to her wishes: "My life had been planned and its course charted by my parents and relatives" (86). Whether she liked it or not, she was sentenced to a life of domesticity with a man who was "thin, walking with a stoop and had bad teeth." And, as she tells us, "Until my wedding night I did not have the slightest knowledge of what went on between men and women in the process of procreation" (24). Not surprising, therefore, her relationship with her husband "was like a chieftain who collected the taxes due to him from his vassal, simply and without exhilaration" (98).

This husband, being much older and more experienced in the ways of the world than his wife, tried to mold her in a manner that suited him. He represents the oppressive patriarchal society which wishes to see women only in submissive roles:

> Dress in sarees, be girl
> Be wife, they said. Be embroiderer, be cook,
> Be quarreller with servants. Fit in. Oh,
> Belong, cried the categorizers. Don't sit
> On walls or peep in through our lace-draped windows.
> Be Amy, or be Kamala. Or, better
> Still, be Madhavikutty. It is time to
> Choose a name, a role. Don't play pretending games.
>
> ["An Introduction"]

Marriage places before a woman a set of gender-defined roles inscribed by society. Transgressing these roles is tantamount to a defiance of social norms and invites the wrath of the power-holders, in this case the men. Reality, for the society is only what it chooses to see, and it chooses to see women in certain fixed roles. That alone is normal while any deviation is seen as "playing games," as abnormal. And thus is a woman forced to wear a mask throughout her life, whether she relishes it or not:

> I must pose,
> I must pretend,
> I must act the role
> Of happy woman,
> Happy wife. ["The Suicide"]

This is how society wishes to see its women: as happy wives and mothers content in the greater glory of father / husband / lover. Women have no business to be discontented with their lot. Kamala Das, however, protests:

> Woman, is this happiness, this lying buried
> Beneath a man? It's time again to come alive,
> The world extends a lot beyond his six foot frame.
> ["The Conflagration"]

The idea of being buried alive, of being smothered in a claustrophobic world, runs through the poetry and she longs to escape from it:

> I shall some day leave, leave the cocoon
> You built around me with morning tea,
> Love-words flung from doorways and of course,
> Your tired lust. I shall some day take
> Wings, fly around, as often petals
> Do when free in air. ["I Shall Some Day"]

The desired movement is from captivity to liberation as a woman (wife, rather) seeks her own space. It is captivity in the domestic set-up that the poet finds dissatisfying. It does have love in some form, but only in the form of tidbits, only as a jaded, indifferent emotion. This is the kind of sentiment, present in most Indian arranged marriages, that keeps a woman duty-bound to her home. It may provide security, at the same time "secures" her firmly to a place patriarchy inscribes for her. There are few other options available to her.

Beneath the rebellious facade of the poems lurks the true poet who is actually timid and withdrawn, a sensitive individual who is hurt and intimidated when society criticizes her, wondering whether or not she was "normal":

> I asked my husband,
> am I hetero
> am I lesbian
> or am I just plain frigid?
> He only laughed.
> For such questions
> probably there are no answers
> or else
> the answers must emerge
> from within. ["Composition"]

Seeking an answer to these unanswered questions, she sometimes concludes that possibly she must be abnormal:

> I am a freak. It's only
> To save my face, I flaunt, at
> Times, a grand, flamboyant lust. ["The Freaks"]

At times Das would like to opt for the more conventional path and return to tradition, as in *My Story* the narrative turns a full circle when she returns home to Nalapat. But that is another phase, another attitude she adopts. This particular choice, to return to the ancestral home (the return symbolizing an acceptance of patriarchal power) is sometimes taken as uncharacteristic of the poet who shows a continual tendency to defy social laws and customs in ways that are flamboyant, even volatile. So the return to convention, to roots and tradition, is seen a mere ploy aimed at the more conventional reader who would find it morally satisfying to see a prodigal turn back home. Whatever it may be, this dithering between rebellion and submission is indicative of the pulls and pressures operating upon a woman, now provoking her into rebellion and then, again, compelling her to surrender.

Das's subject is heterosexual relationships. For Kamala Das, communication is important in any relationship. "I wanted conversation, companionship, and warmth," she says candidly at one point (87). One may communicate on one level through the intellect, the mind and the soul. At another, one communicates on the physical plane, through the body. Kamala Das focuses attention on the body and its needs, and how it needs to communicate with the outside world through the windows of its various senses. And yet, the body is also the means by which women are exploited the most when sexual relationship is reduced to a mere "skin-communicated thing" and love and tenderness are replaced by lust and authoritarianism. The body, in other words, becomes a territory which may be conquered by hostile male forces. Not surprising, therefore, the physical form arouses ambivalent emotions in the poet. Sometimes she is overcome with awe at its beauty and dignity; she loves it, talks about it, even celebrates it. The female body is beautiful, especially in the context of a satisfactory sexual relationship:

> Gift him all,
> Gift him what makes you woman, the scent of
> Long hair, the musk of sweat between the breasts,
> The warm shock of menstrual blood, and all your
> Endless female hungers. ["The Looking Glass"]

On other occasions, generally when she thinks of how dependent the responses of a woman's body are to male stimulus, she seems to feel almost a loathing for it:

> ...You were pleased
> With my body's response, its weather, its usual shallow
> Convulsions. You dribbled spittle into my mouth, you poured

Yourself into every nook and cranny....
["The Old Playhouse"]

Evident in these lines is a disgust for the physical needs of the body which may not necessarily be attributed to a lack of desire but to a failure of achieving fulfilment in sexual relationship. In marriage such a lop-sided relationship is like that between the conqueror and the conquered, the colonizer and the colonized, always with the woman as victim.

Does she speak purely of her personal experiences? Perhaps. But, although she begins with the personal, her story may be extended to include all unhappy women:

You planned to tame a swallow, to hold her
In the long summer of your love, so that she would forget
Not the raw seasons alone, and the home left behind but
Also her nature, the urge to fly and the endless
Pathways of the sky. ["The Old Playhouse"]

Her concern is not only with her personal predicament but with that of all women trapped in a love/marriage relationship which refuses to let them grow as independent entities. She seems to address no one particular man but all men in general who take for granted that women must play a subservient role and that their lives must revolve around their male partner. "Cowering / beneath your monstrous ego I ate the magic loaf and / became a dwarf," says she in "The Old Playhouse." She must live her life as a pigmy, in the shadow of a husband who looms large over her life. It is his world in which she has been condescendingly given a small, inconsequential place.

Kamala Das's attempt is to move from margin to center, from a position of little or no consequence to one which is crucial to her world. Hence, through her poems she shifts her focus from woman as the representative of patriarchal power to her woman as a separate self. In a bid to tell the male world that she cares little for them or their authority, she narcissistically turns to herself:

I must let my mind striptease
I must extrude
autobiography. ["Composition"]

Which brings us back to the same question: is it "autobiography" that she tells? In fact it is the story of every woman caught in a hostile socio-cultural environment, and in dissatisfying relationships. Elsewhere she does say, "I am every / Woman who seeks love" ("An Introduction"). When indulging in her "striptease" she is in the process of shedding all that is grossly physical, trying to transcend it and reach a plane where the temporal intersects the timeless, where it is the eternal human spirit that matters, not this perishable body with its transient desires:

...by confessing
by peeling off my layers
I reach closer to the soul ["Composition"]

Throughout her poetic career, Kamala Das has devoted herself to exclusively one subject: herself. And she has written on just one theme: love. She has spoken of herself because she is convinced that the only authentic poetry is about one's own self. And she wrote about love because with her it was an undying obsession. She never abandoned the romantic quest for true love. Her poems trace her unwavering journey in its pursuit. Perhaps one may detect a degree of naiveté in her belief in love as a means of salvation: naiveté that borders on immaturity. With time one would expect some evolution in her poetic themes or attitudes, but not in the case of Kamala Das. As Vrinda Nabar tells us in her insightful study of the poet, "What appeals to and disturbs us... is the seeming inability to learn from experience, to withdraw, to show restraint. The poet is like a moth which, having singed itself, must still fly into the flame, till it is destroyed completely" [Nabar 62-63]. Das shows a single-mindedness in the pursuit of her themes which remain unchanged despite minor variations.

When Kamala Das was still a child, an idea that formed in her impressionable mind was that of love being a form of devotion, a prayer, or *tapasya*. To some extent she traces the origin of this concept to her aunt Ammini who voluntarily chose the life of an ascetic and spent much of her time alone: "...she sat on the window sill and recited the love-songs written by Kumaranasan, whose poetry was fashionable then. It was while listening to her voice that I sensed for the first time that love was a beautiful anguish and a tapasya" (14). The message passed on from the aunt to the niece was this romantic notion of the oneness of pleasure and pain, of love and anguish. Out of this romantic delusion the impressionable Kamala Das would perhaps never emerge. It is also likely that the aunt appealed to Kamala Das for more than one reason: in the first place, she (the aunt) was a rebel against the givens of the culture, defying the institution of matrimony and preferring to stay single. Secondly, through her songs she pointed to an alternative path that one could follow, to the self-contained world of the imagination where one may be free of social bondage. This was the rebel's path. And yet it was a form of rebellion against the domestic code that was socially acceptable. For a woman who renounced pleasures of the flesh and chose an ascetic life could pose no danger to its laws, even if she recited love-poetry and lived in an unreal, imaginary world. She would not set an objectionable, dangerous, or "immoral" precedent to others.

Influenced by her aunt, Kamala Das would lose herself in romantic reverie: "I thought then that love was flowers in the hair, it was the yellow moon lighting up a familiar face and soft words whispered in the ear" (93). In marriage she had expected to find the fulfilment of a romantic fantasy: "I had expected him to take me in his arms and stroke my hair, my hands and whisper loving words" (87). She would imagine her mate to be the ideal one, a god of sorts. As she tells us, "It was to get closer to that bodiless one that I approached other forms and lost my way. I may have gone astray but not once did I forget my destination" (124). And, again: "My mate is He. He shall come to me in myriad shapes. In many shapes shall I surrender to His desire" (197). But even though she "looked for the beauteous Krishna in every man," [Singh:15] she hastens to remove any possible misunderstanding, saying that there is nothing unnatural in this search for the ideal partner because "Every Hindu girl is in reality wedded to Lord Krishna." [Ibid.]

> Vrindavan lives on in every woman's mind,
> And the flute, luring her
> From home and her husband.

In her autobiography, she repeats the same point, "Through the smoke of the incense I saw the beauteous smile of my Krishna. Always, always, I shall love you I told him, not speaking aloud but willing him to hear me, only you will be my husband, only your horoscope will match with mine" (96).

Lord Krishna symbolizes ideal love: the kind that is handed down through myths and legends. Kamala Das envisages herself surrendering completely at the altar of the most amorous of Indian gods:

> Everything in me
> Is melting, even the hardness at the core.
> O Krishna. I'm melting, melting, melting,
> Nothing remains but
> You....

in lines that remind us of St. Augustine's chant of "burning burning burning" [?] repeated by T. S. Eliot in *The Waste Land*. And, indeed, there are parallels between Kamala Das's story and that of St. Augustine who, after a wayward youth, decided to turn to God.

> Your body is my prison, Krishna,
> I cannot see beyond it.
> Your darkness blinds me.
> Your love words shut out the wise world's din.
>
> ["Krishna"]

Even when she was totally obsessed with the love of another man,

Kamala Das remained preoccupied with the legend of Krishna and his *gopis*. She would imagine them wailing for him: "O Krishna, Oh Kanhaiya, do not leave me for another."

This image of a woman pining for her divine lover has its roots in the Mirabai tradition. Mirabai, as the legend goes, was devoted to Lord Krishna even though he was married to another woman, and even though he was involved in amorous adventures with a number of women. Mirabai's attachment to Krishna is, however, acceptable to the conservative Indian mind as she transforms sexual desire into a religious fervor. Das's references to Krishna are generally in connection with his pursuit of Radha, but the devotion she describes is more the self-negating Mira's than the more fortunate Radha for whom Krishna actually showed a preference. Radha's contentment in love is thus fused with Mira's self-surrender as Kamala Das describes what is obviously an obsession with a man as a sort of holy trance which transcends all that is banal. It is some such total sacrifice that Das is trying to evoke in her poems when she speaks of a complete surrender in love. Her effort, initially, was to surrender herself to human love. But when it came under social censure, she transformed her attention from human love to divine. This is how Kamala Das becomes a devotee of Krishna on whose legends she had thrived as a child. Doing so, she indirectly turns her back on herself as a responsible, free-thinking adult, and opts for childhood once more, going back to the legends that the grown-up world used to feed her on. Ironically, she is once again defining herself in terms of values and traditions handed down to her by the patriarchal set-up, thus conceding the superiority of their world and the inadequacy of her own.

At this point it becomes interesting to ponder what exactly Kamala Das has achieved by turning away from one form of love (the husband's, the lovers') to another (Krishna's). Has she not cast off one kind of bondage only to take on another? For here, again, figures the language of the prisoner: "Your body is my *prison*," she says, admitting her incarcerated state. And again the claustrophobic images of blinding and darkness, of being shut away from everything else. The only difference is that earlier it was *physical* love which held her captive. Now physical relationship, that "skin-communicated thing" has been dispensed with and what obsesses the woman is spiritual love. But (and this is a point not to be missed!) in both cases there is a total surrender of the self. The option chosen later is nothing if not one approved of by patriarchy in the sense that it is a *male* god and one who traditionally has a horde of female admirers around him. Kamala Das who, in *My Story*, found it distasteful when her husband was surrounded by admiring female relatives herself becomes a devotee of Krishna. Doing so she is, in a way, voluntarily opting for what is undeniably a state of vassaldom.

This is a significant aspect of the poet's revolt against a society which marginalizes its women by repeatedly ensuring their silence, their docility and passivity. Hers is a revolt that fails, for while rejecting one set of male values, she inadvertently opts for another which, paradoxically, is equally male-oriented, equally humiliating to women. Had she followed what she said was her true "nature," to fly like the swallow, she would probably have arrived at a different conclusion. The answer to the dilemmas that women face do not lie in the passivity of a Mira Bai, or in the rigors of an ascetic's life. The peculiarities of their individual needs and desires demand a different response, keeping in mind the interests of the female community. Kamala Das could have been a torch-bearer, the Indian counterpart of someone like Adrienne Rich. But she never really understood what the feminist movement was all about, as may be discerned from an almost irresponsible statement she once made:

> Off and on I too toy with the idea of joining the Women's Lib movement, if only to have the fun of walking around with no bra on. Such a delicious pleasure! But you must do it only when there are several men around to throw admiring glances to your full-blown beauty. Otherwise you might as well wear the wretched thing and forget about the movement.
>
> [*Blitz*, March 12, 1977, p.15]

Besides, she chose to buckle under the pressures of the oppressive society and went back on the rebellion she had initiated. She turned back to tradition, ultimately viewing herself not as a misfit but as part of the society. Although she vociferously claims that she does not regret writing *My Story* (Interview 167), she makes one lame excuse after another to explain why it was written: excuses which contradict her intention to "disturb the society" out of its complacence. For instance she says that she wrote it to pay hospital bills, or that she wrote it because her husband told her to do so for the money it would bring. All these contradictions are symptomatic: they indicate the true nature of the poet who was a rebel, no doubt, but one placed in a counter-current of social pressures which slowly but surely took their toll on the defiant individual spirit.

Poetry in Times of Terror: Anna Akhmatova

> In the fearful years of the Yezhov terror I spent seventeen months in prison queues in Leningrad. One day somebody 'identified' me. Beside me, in the queue, there was a woman with blue lips. She had, of course, never heard of me; but she suddenly came out of that trance so common to us all and whispered in my ear (everybody spoke in whispers there): 'Can you describe this?' And I said : 'Yes, I can.' And then something like the shadow of a smile crossed what had once been her face.
>
> Anna Akhmatova. 1 April 1957, Leningrad

The Russian poet Anna Akhmatova (1889-1966) is unlike Adrienne Rich who visualizes communities of women. She is also unlike Margaret Atwood whose poems speak loud and clear of gender politics, or Stevie Smith who is full of venom against an irresponsible father. In fact she is unlike any of the feminist stereotypes that we as readers and critics are by now accustomed to. Anna Akhmatova forces us to revise our concept of women's poetry which is mainly derived from Anglo-American and French Feminist thought. Through her poetry she highlights the limitations of feminist theories which do not take into consideration the creative work of a woman in times of political repression. Western feminist theories have more or less confined themselves to women's immediate experiences in relation to men, generally in the domestic and personal sphere. They have attempted to analyze the conditioning of the female psyche by a predominantly patriarchal society, they have focused on the denial of equal rights and opportunities to women, and the subtle undermining of their status in a countless number of ways. These are primarily theoretical considerations which have not taken into account the actual life-experiences of a woman which cannot be textualized, or which cannot be reduced to a given formula. Feminist concepts have emerged out of primarily non-political contexts where state repression did not figure. Thus they prove inadequate when confronted with reality of a different kind. For instance, how would a woman react when the state intrudes into her individual life and attempts to distort her creative talent? When the public order impinges on her private life, weighs down on her oppressively, tries to condition her very thoughts, denying her the outlet of expression? The work of the Russian poet, Anna Akhmatova, highlights these gaps in our perception of women's poetry and illustrates that poetry by women may reach out beyond gender concerns to embrace much larger issues involving the experiences, the rights and duties of citizens in a time of political turmoil and repression.

Anna Andreyevna Gorenko, who later became Anna Akhmatova and penned moving songs about the sufferings and humiliations of her people, was born in the year 1889. Her talent flowered at a time when not only the literary but also the political scene in Russia was in ferment. She, with her companions, broke away from the existing Symbolist way of writing and, experimenting with a new kind of poetry, became one of the leading exponents of the "Acmeist" movement which emerged in 1910. Other poets associated with this group were her first husband, Nikolai Gumilev, and Osip Mandelstam, a trusted friend. The movement did not survive long as it was smothered by the political upheavals of the country. Gumilev was executed in 1921, Mandelstam spent the rest of his life in concentration camps, and Akhmatova herself, grappling with the terror of the State, continued to write bitter poems on the Russian war and Revolution. She wrote of her times, of her people and their agony. She wrote of death, "the Noseless Slut" ("Poem Without a Hero"), waiting at every corner. She wrote of how it felt to be nameless and faceless, one of the endless serpentine hordes queuing up outside a Leningrad prison, hoping in vain for some news of a loved one.

The Stalinist regime considered Akhmatova's commitment to

the people dangerous. It executed her first husband and transported her son to Siberia. Her own movements were severely curtailed. She was considered a suspect and had secret police agents dogging all her moves. The State tried to silence her with a paltry old-age pension when she was barely in her thirties. Akhmatova reacted by lapsing into a long silence. After the death of Stalin, however, came gradual rehabilitation and she lived long enough to be considered a spokesman for all Russia. She won the hearts of her countrymen and was praised by her contemporaries – Pasternak, Mandelstam, and Tsvetaeva. When she died in 1966, she was at the height of her fame and the streets of Leningrad swarmed with her admirers who had come to mourn. Today her work is regarded as a cultural monument to the period which "encompasses two world wars, a revolution, a civil war, the Stalinist purges, the cold war and the thaw. She was able to create her own understanding of that period by finding symbolic significance in her own fate and in that of those close to her who embodied some or other aspect of the general situation" [Rosslyn 1].

Anna Akhmatova stands apart from other women poets. What makes her unlike the others? True, she does seem to write a very different kind of poetry, but what keeps her apart is not simply her versification but her perception, her vision of the world. At first gender concerns do not seem to be her primary interest. It is as a Russian woman that Akhmatova writes: a Russian living through turbulent times that negated the very identity of the individual, whether male or female. The poems of Akhmatova are written against a particular temporal and spatial framework. The focus is on the first half of the twentieth century, a period of transition with all its upheavals and their far-reaching consequences. The space the poems occupy is the Soviet Union that was – the country which lived through and survived the Stalinist terror and struggled through great economic and social revolution. This is the background. Against this fixed chronotopic situation are foregrounded related concerns which move the poet.

Akhmatova's work is different from that of Marina Tsvetaeva (1892-1941) who remained more of an outcast whether she was in exile or in Russia, an émigré poet writing in the loneliness of poverty and exile, trying in vain to fight losing battles and finally, in desperation, dying by her own hand. Akhmatova had more grit and tenacity. Throughout her poetic career she remained in Russia, braving the onslaughts on her individuality. It is evident that hers was not an easy life. In fact it was a life full of struggles. Akhmatova's is the story of a thinking woman pitted against a world hostile to her deepest aspirations, living within a system that was not yet ready to recognize or accept her for what she was. And yet she remained undaunted, committed to her vocation.

> No, not under the vault of alien skies,
> And not under the shelter of alien wings –
> I was with my people then,
> There, where my people, unfortunately, were.
>
> [Akhmatova II:95]

This tenacity of purpose, this obstinacy, is an important characteristic of the poet and the person. Even when life was intolerable in Russia, when others in her situation jumped at the first opportunity to get out of the country, Akhmatova dug in her heels and refused to emigrate. It was as a Russian that she identified herself and Russian would she remain: a Russian rooted in her own soil, even though this rootedness involved untold pain and sorrow.

The paradigm that often surfaces in Akhmatova's poems is that of a binary opposition between power and powerlessness, oppression and submission, the victimizer and the victimized. Invariably, the victim is a nameless commoner suffering the atrocities of a callous regime, trying to survive despite all onslaughts on his physical, emotional, and mental being. It is a woman's point of view that Akhmatova presents, a woman living in times of fear and terror, reacting to the political situation. Sometimes, placed against the political backdrop are gender issues which get intermeshed with political ones. In her personal life, as Anna Andreyevna, the poet was just another Russian citizen hounded by the state. In her poetry, Russian politics are interwoven with sexual politics so that it is not easy to distinguish the one from the other. Inevitably, the study of the one includes an involvement with the other.

For Akhmatova, hurdles in life started early. At first it was her father who objected to his name being associated with poetry. And so Anna Andreyevna Gorenko became Anna Akhmatova, taking on the name of her Tartar grandmother. The choice of the assumed name is significant, pointing as it does to the unconscious affinity the poet felt with a female ancestor who provided solace when the patriarchal world let her down. Not that her father considered her writing worthless – in fact he actually thought she wrote well – but he simply objected to her use of his name. It did not seem necessary to give any reason for this whim but the implication is clear: the achievement of a woman would, perhaps, show up the patriarch at a disadvantage, as a lesser talent, may be. Perhaps, there is an underlying unconscious resentment of a female offspring vying for pinnacles of name and fame which the parent has not been able to reach. Hence the condescension: she may be allowed to write but the patriarchal world would have nothing to do with it, would own no responsibility. This condescending attitude towards Akhmatova was later to be adopted by Stalin's regime.

After the father's grudging assent to her poetry, came the men who tried to shape the poet in their own mold. First her suitor, Gumilev, who became her first husband. Gumilev it was who introduced Akhmatova to the literary world and published her first poems. It was with him that she met other leading Russian writers, Pasternak, Mandelstam, Tsvetaeva, Anrep, and others. His role as a husband, and their shared experiences, inspired many of her poems. With him, hers was a sheltered life. Her poems of this early period, *Evening* (1912), and *Rosary* (1914), speak of love and personal relationships. Ostensibly this was a time of heady success, of shared interests and achievements. A rude awakening was soon to follow.

The early love poems of Akhmatova are fairly predictable. In one of them she depicts love as a hangman, implying that love and pain co-exist: in order to experience love one has to pay a certain price. This is an integral part of gender politics. A poem from *Evening* is worth looking at as an illustration of an early theme:

He loved three things in life:
Evensong, white peacocks,
And old maps of America.
He hated it when children cried,
He hated tea with raspberry jam
And woman's hysterics.
... And I was his wife. [I: 261]

A poem like this, which brings out the polarities between the male world dominated by intellectual work and aesthetic considerations and the female world of domestic drudgery, does not seem to be much different from that by any other woman caught in an unsatisfactory marriage relationship. Written in 1911, it is a far cry from the later poetry of Akhmatova. Perhaps, if circumstances had been different, if Akhmatova had made her home in a country other than Russia, if a totalitarian state had not usurped individual rights and liberties in Russia, her poetry would have taken a different course. It would have traveled along predictable roads, spoken of soured personal relationships, of the desire to break free from bonds that constrain, and of the yearning for a perfect state where women could live with respect and dignity and not as domestic charwomen. In other words, her poetry would have been , perhaps, like that of Adrienne Rich, or Sylvia Plath, or any other woman poet of the century. But this was not to be.

Akhmatova's early poems seem to be quite conventional. The theme is generally love: love tragic or unrequited. There are the usual vacillations between the high and the low, between despair and elation, depending on the mood changes of the lover. An example of the early themes would be the poem "Reading Hamlet" which deals with another instance of unrequited love where the Prince tells Ophelia to go to a nunnery or marry a fool.

You told me: "All right then, get thee to a nunnery,
Or go get married to a fool..."
Only princes make such speeches,
But I remembered those words. [I:279]

The implications are clear: the choices facing Akhmatova's woman, like those of the love-crazed Ophelia, are limited. She may, if she wishes, still pursue the Prince, even though he spurns her; she may withdraw from the world of men and retreat into a convent as a nun; or she may get married to a fool (implying that only a fool would marry a woman who has loved another man). Akhmatova's poem is an illustration of how male values – symbolized by Hamlet's cruel remarks to Ophelia – may be internalized by women and accepted without a protest.

Biographical accounts tell us that Akhmatova was emotionally blackmailed into her marriage with Gumilev. Gumilev would threaten to take his life if she did not marry him, and several times attempted suicide. Finally, worn out by his entreaties, Akhmatova married him and entered into what she saw was the "beginning of the end" of their relationship. Dissatisfaction followed on both sides. In marrying a woman he had long fantasized about, Gumilev's expectations were far from real. A poem by him says:

> I took not a wife but a witch.
> I thought her amusing
> Guessed she might be capricious,
> A gay and happy song bird.
>
> You call out and she frowns
> You hug her and she bristles
> When the moon comes out she starts pining....
>
> [Gumilev, Haight 16]

The power of suggestion was so great that Akhmatova actually started judging herself by his yardstick, viewing herself as a witch, a wicked woman, a bad mother. Initially there was self-recrimination with reference to Gumilev, then to her son, and then it lingered on long after she had walked out of the claustrophobic marriage. Even with her second husband, Shileyko with whom she had a brief but stormy marriage, there were problems: "You do not want children from me / And you do not love my poems" [I. 186]. Thus wrote

Akhmatova. The problem lies, in both cases, in the inability of the male partners to accept the creative powers of the woman, in their unwillingness to recognize their genius, and in their insistent desire to "possess". As a poem by Akhmatova put it:

> He whispers "I am not sorry
> For loving you this way –
> Either be mine alone
> Or I will kill you."
>
> [I:559]

As Akhmatova poetry evolved, the scenario changed. The world in which Anna Akhmatova lived passed through the throes of a tumultuous revolution and nothing was ever the same. As a later poem described it, it became a world where miracles could no longer take place because men and women no longer had any faith:

> Now no one will listen to songs.
> The prophesied days have begun.
> Latest poem of mine, the world has lost its wonder,
> Don't break my heart, don't ring out. [I:519]

Akhmatova was a witness to the end of an era, an era of innocence, and the irrevocable onset of a reality which augured misery and sorrow for the masses. In times like this, when Russia became "an old peasant / Killing his meat" (*Anno Domini*), when she saw that "The Russian earth loves, loves / Droplets of blood" (*Ibid.*), how could a poet possibly continue to sing of love and personal relationships? The issues that mattered were broader-based. The songs that were needed were of a different kind.

Whereas much of the love poetry was written when Akhmatova's was still an innocent world, before the violence of the 1917 revolution changed the face of Russia, after the outbreak of the revolution the focus of Akhmatova's poetry shifted from personal relationships to the relationships of people to the times, turbulent times of uncertainty and fear. The hangman is no longer love but something else that must remain unnamed. It is an all-pervasive, coercive power that curtails the liberty of individuals and forces them into silence. There is, thus, a move from private poetry to one that is committed to public events and experiences. Akhmatova would like to tell us the truth of the times in which she lived and suffered. She would like to tell us what it was like to live in those terrible times. But, because of the oppressive conditions in which she lived, she could not do so directly. So, like Emily Dickinson, she told the truth, but told it slant. One may read her poems and try to figure what lies between the lines, how much of the truth is hidden, understated or left unsaid.

In 1917, the year in which Lenin and the Bolsheviks came to power, began a new chapter in Akhmatova's life when she and Gumilev separated. The country was caught in the throes of political unrest, with the Civil War beginning in 1919. All opponents of the new regime were hounded and persecuted. For Akhmatova, the reign of Terror began in 1921. Innocence made way for experience as the very texture of life changed in Russia, not only for Akhmatova, but for all its people. Nothing would ever be the same. Akhmatova shifted her attention from the love lyrics of *Rosary* to solemn and austere poems on the Russian war and revolution (*Anno Domini*, 1922). Stalin came to power in 1924 and the Reign of Terror in Russia continued in full swing. Resistance to Stalin's regime was met with mass persecutions, deportations and other forms of repression. Akhmatova continued to write although she did not publish any poems in Russia from 1925 to 1940.

In Stalin's animosity toward writers one may read a fear psychosis: a fear of the power of the pen which, proverbially, is mightier than the sword. One may see reflected in this attitude an irrational fear of emotions, of sentiments and feelings, and of all those who believe in giving expression to them. This attitude is not new. Plato, one may recall, was suspicious of poetry and banned most of its types from his Republic. According to him (*Republic*, Bk. 10), the state must not only protect its citizens against the corrupting influence of meretricious poetry but also indoctrinate them in virtue. Significantly, he permitted those poets to remain who sang "praises of gods and encomia of famous men" (*Republic* 10.607). Plato's views on the power of poetry partly contributed to the idea of the poet being the voice of the masses and a spokesman for nationalist feelings. In other words, the poet is a power to reckon with. This is also the reason why poetry, the voice of the poet, with its power to move and educate the masses is treated with suspicion. So it is suspect in the eyes of a totalitarian state. Poetry, by arousing the emotions, leads people astray. In this connection it may be noted that emotions, feelings, and sentiments are abstracts states which denote passivity, generally considered a feminine condition, opposed to activity, virility, and vigor, traditionally looked upon as male characteristics. Stalin's regime seemed to suffer from some such obsessions, hence the persecution of writers and poets. Not that the state was merciful towards male poets. On the flimsiest of pretexts they were arrested and imprisoned or executed. This is what happened to Osip Mandelstam who died in a concentration camp, and Gumilev who was accused of being a counter-revolutionary and executed in 1921. Although Akhmatova was by then divorced from Gumilev, she knew that to some extent their former relationship was the reason for his doom, just as her relationship with the Mandelstams was probably responsible for his sad end. Her son, Lev Gumilev, spent a major portion of his life in transit camps. His fault? Only that he was the offspring of a woman who had a voice, who wrote poems. Her own misfortunes, too, needless to say, Akhmatova attributed "to Stalin's personal paranoia" [Berlin 48].

If one were to enumerate the state's charges against Akhmatova, the first and foremost unspecified charge, undoubtedly, was that she was a poet. A poet is one who has the ability to transform feelings and experiences into words, one who knows how to give a voice and expression to what is happening in the world, one who has the gift of language. In an autocratic regime the existence of such vocal subjects does not suit the ruling party's interests. An ideal populace for a totalitarian state is a faceless, voiceless one that will carry orders without a murmur. Silence is, thus, a precondition for such a government or else its authority is threatened. This was Akhmatova's unpardonable fault: she was born with a voice while the state wanted her to be mute. When she spoke she was heard and supported by millions, but the powers in control wanted her to remain silent lest she should undermine their authority. Her fault was further compounded by her marriage to Gumilev, another poet. So, she was a double threat. Moreover, together, the two had established the "Acmeist" movement with other poets and writers. No doubt this was a literary movement aiming at the promotion of art and culture, but for the state it had dangerous overtones and it simply had to be nipped in the bud. So, from 1925 until 1940, Akhmatova lapsed into a self-imposed silence. Her works were not published even though she continued to write in private. In 1946 the Central Committee of the Communist Party initiated action against the magazines *Zvezda* (*Star*) and *Leningrad* for publishing Akhmatova's work. Zhdanov, who was the much-feared aide of Stalin, passed a decree banning Akhmatova's poetry for "poisoning the minds of the youth." In 1949, when her son, Lev, was re-arrested, she thought of resorting to a compromise to help him: she tried to play along with the oppressor and wrote a cycle of poems, "In Praise of Peace" (1950), in praise of Stalin's regime. These are propagandist poems which she wrote against her better judgment and she did not want to hand them down to posterity. For this reason, she did not wish to include them in her collected works.

Akhmatova, in her poetry, focuses on her own experiences and attitudes. What emerges indirectly is a fairly accurate portrayal of herself. She comes across neither as the Virgin nor as a whore, but realistically, and could easily represent womanhood in general. In one poem she depicts herself as an inconspicuous figure, neither glamorous nor drab:

> Neither shepherdess not queen
> And no longer a nun, I –
>
> In this everyday gray dress,
> On rundown heels...
> But, as before, the burning embrace,
> The same fear in enormous eyes. [I:343, 45]

And in Poem IV of *Requiem* she addresses herself as the "Gay little sinner of Tsarkoye Selo." The realism in her self-depiction is obvious. She does not give us an idealized picture of herself. She does not place herself on a pedestal. Nor is there any bitterness or apology or self-recrimination towards herself. Somewhat cynical, perhaps, she is able to turn her gaze inward impartially and present a faithful picture of herself. It is this realism that she would like others to imbibe in their attitude towards women. But, for this very reason, perhaps, ironic though it seems, she herself could not escape such stereotyped censure: unsympathetic critics treated her as a dubious hybrid, something in between a nun and a whore! She was described as "a nun who crosses herself as she kisses her beloved" [Haight, p. 69], or a "half 'harlot' burning with passion, half mendicant nun able to pray to God for forgiveness" [Ibid. 72]. Andrey Zhdanov, better known as Stalin's cultural watchdog, branded her "not quite nun, not quite a harlot, but rather a harlot and a nun, whose fornication is mixed with prayer" [Rosslyn 11]. This censure was based on the 1923 harsh comments of the critic, Boris Eichenbaum, on the co-existence of the sensual and the spiritual in the work of Akhmatova, the manner in which she combines mystical experiences with the spiritual. Whatever the logic behind them, these are sexist judgments born of a false belief in male superiority.

With time, Akhmatova's poetry came into its own as she defined more clearly the themes that moved her. Love, dreams and other sentimental subjects took a backseat and the focus shifted to hard reality: the problems being faced by the country and her people. But even though the poet grew concerned with the affairs of the state, she remained aware of the need to hold on to her own poetic integrity. This is evident from her poem entitled *Poema Bez Geroya (Poem Without a Hero)*, a more or less autobiographical piece with which she remained obsessed from 1940 almost to the end of her life. The title of the poem is significant and underscores the fact that Akhmatova was no longer the dreamy, sentimental, lovelorn poet of the early poems. Time and experience taught her that she no longer needed to define her existence in relationship to men, lovers or husbands. The poem was written when Akhmatova was in the most depressing of circumstances which included poverty, ill-health, and official repression. There were times when she feared losing her mental equilibrium. Coping with the situation the best she could, she tried to divert her mind to other thoughts, to another time, another world. The fruit of her efforts, *Poem Without a Hero*, gripped her like a fever, like bouts of an incurable illness, and she wrote and rewrote it all the time.

Ostensibly a love poem to her city, Petersburg (Leningrad), it attempts to re-capture certain events of the year 1913 that Anna Akhmatova and her companions lived through. In particular, it recreates a tragedy that had a tremendous impact on the poet: the suicide of a young officer, Vsevolod Knyazev, who was also a minor poet, on the doorstep of Olga Sudeikina, one of the city beauties. *Poem Without a Hero* tries to come to terms with the tragedy, pondering over its senselessness. Apart from the *femme fatale* and her paramour, there are other men and women mentioned in this poem and they all people a private world that the poet and her few friends were familiar with. Apparently there is no hero but implicit in the title is the existence of a heroine who is none other than the poet. It is her perception and sensibility that is recorded in the poem. More than a re-creation of Petersburg's "Silver Age" (as it was called) it is a statement of the mind that perceives rather than the scene that is described. The very fact that Akhmatova moves back in time to focus on an irretrievably lost past, rather than a troublesome present, suggests an incipient rebellion against the present repressive regime. By turning towards the year 1913 Akhmatova is turning her back on 1940 and onward, on Stalin and his cronies, on the privations of the times. She is asserting herself in this oblique manner, her muse coming to her aid.

Living in circumstances peculiar to her age and time, it is not surprising that Akhmatova's writing displays certain special characteristics: it has a heightened intensity of feeling, as though uncertain of what the morrow may bring. Occasionally, it seems to harbor a passivity and helplessness in the face of given situations, almost as though the poet were contemplating the futility of trying to fight a pre-ordained future. And often it seems to believe in fate or destiny. Perhaps this is not an escapist or defeatist attitude because there is a transcendental movement in the poems: the poet trying to rise above the harshness of lived experience to focus on the intellectual fruits of poetry. Akhmatova moves towards a self-contained attitude that would not care if the world thought her to be a witch:

> Before me in this chamber lived
> A solitary sorceress:
> Her shadow is still visible
> On the eve of the new moon....
> She glances at me.
> I am not one of those
> Subject to other people's spells,
> ... But, by the way,
> I don't just give my secrets away. [I. 278]

Akhmatova simply had to travel the long hard road to reach where she finally did. Without going through the grind of male prejudice and political repression, she would not have evolved into the poet she became. She would not be recognized as the literary chronicler of Russia's turbulent times. He stature today is partly dependent on the fact that she raised her voice at a time and in a place where women were not supposed to have a voice, and against powers far too strong for an individual human being to fight against. She re-examined the position of woman in a man-made social world, tried to re-examine male sexist judgments, erase the boundaries between the 'nun' and the 'harlot', the so-called pure and the impure. She did all this at the cost of censure, at the risk of being branded wicked and immoral.

All said and done, the fact remains that Akhmatova could write poetry despite the repressive circumstances she lived in, despite the fact that her physical liberty was curtailed, sources of income were meager or nil, and patronage none. This speaks of the triumph of the mind over matter. Her mind to her was a kingdom that none could vanquish. There she could reign supreme, converting public sorrow and personal grief into songs which other fellow sufferers would hear and understand. Akhmatova did not allow her muse to desert her. She held on to her through good times and bad, knowing her to be her one and only friend. She described her source of inspiration thus:

> When at night I await her coming,
> It seems that life hangs by a strand.
> What are honours, what is youth, what is freedom,
> Compared to that dear guest with rustic pipe in hand?
>
> And she entered. Drawing aside her shawl,
> She gazed attentively at me.
> I said to her: "Was it you who dictated to Dante
> The pages of *The Inferno*?" She replied: "It was I."
> ["The Muse," II:73]

This is the muse who inspired Akhmatova and enabled her to taste the fruit of success. Significantly, she is female. She may be the Demon Poesy for someone like Keats, but she was also Beatrice, beckoning Dante, from the topmost of the stair, opening the doors for a *Vita Nouva*, a new way of life more whole, more perfect than he could ever imagine. For the woman poet, for Akhmatova, too, the muse is a true friend, providing her a solace in time of need, a safe haven remote from all pain and suffering. Thanks to her faithful muse, Akhmatova continued writing poetry. As she said towards the end of her life, "A poet is someone to whom it is impossible to give anything and from whom it is impossible to take anything away" [Naiman 23]. Akhmatova's voice would not be still even though Stalin's regime tried to stifle it by oppressing her physically and mentally, by attacking her where she was most vulnerable, through her loved ones. She survived it all and wrote about it, thus proving that she was not only as poet but also a woman of grit whose spirit could not be broken despite all odds. Jessie Davies, in her biography of the poet, concludes with a quotation from a journal of the period which describes her triumph:

> "The Stalin police state broke on Akhmatova. To the philistine this maybe seems odd – tens of thousands of Ivan-the-

> Terrible guards, armed with all kinds of instruments of torture fell upon this defenceless woman and she turned out to be the stronger. She was victorious over them all. But there is nothing more surprising about that for us. We know that it is always so. The poet's word is more powerful than all the police oppressors. You can't hide it, trample it under foot or kill it." [Davies 133]

Afterword

As a coda, it may be worthwhile to mention the fact that twentieth-century women's poetry shows more concern with content than form. The innovations that take place are in subject matter and theme rather than in style. True, a poet of the 'sixties like Sylvia Plath does go "stitching and unstitching" in the Yeatsean manner, hammering and tinkering at her art, particularly in her early poems. And a contemporary poet like Lyn Hejinian undertakes an elaborate experiment with form, combining the personal with the experimental. But, by and large, attention is focussed on bringing daring themes into poetry. Hence Anne Sexton boldly speaks of menstruation and childbirth, of masturbation and illicit affairs; Margaret Atwood lays bare hidden animosities between the sexes and exposes conflicts that were earlier conveniently brushed under the carpet; Stevie Smith, like Sylvia Plath and Anne Sexton, strips the patriarchal figure of his authority, asserting an independent viewpoint; Kamala Das brings female desire into her work in explicit terms, flaunting her sexuality; and Anna Akhmatova strikes a still different note, speaking as she does in an undeniably woman's voice trapped in times of political repression. The underlying urge in all their writings seems to be the urge to tell the truth – the truth as it appears to them. Living in the comparatively liberated twentieth century, they were more fortunate than Emily Dickinson and did not have to tell it "slant." And yet the "straight" truth had as many different versions as individuals so that no two poets are alike. Each of the five female voices studied here expresses a unique vision.

In their effort to move the female persona from the margin to the center, the self that emerges is generally in the first person, and so the writing takes on a confessional tone, as one may witness in the poetry of the 'sixties. Often, however, confession is a mask donned by the poet whose attempt is not simply to draw attention to the self, but a self that is representative of the larger species. Autobiography deftly combines with a personally constructed mythology and poetry becomes a fabric of multiple weave – a number of stories being told simultaneously, none more privileged than the others. For example, when H.D. re-tells the story of Helen of Troy, she is engaged in a variety of tasks: *Helen in Egypt* re-visions the story of the exceptionally beautiful woman who has been taken as little more than a *femme fatale*. It rescues from oblivion a version of the story – that by Stesichorus – which presents Helen in a more charitable light. At the same time, *Helen in Egypt* is re-visionist because it presents the author herself from a totally new perspective: not just as the Imagist poet whose work was overshadowed by heavyweight contemporaries like T.S. Eliot, Ezra Pound, and William Carlos Williams but as a feminist poet concerned with the female quest for identity, examining a woman's plight in a patriarchal society, the injustices she is often subjected to, and her long and arduous journey towards an individual voice, towards self-realization and fulfillment. It is such a journey, that is charted in different ways in poetry written by women in the twentieth century.

As may be surmised, this study of twentieth-century women's poetry is by no means complete. Analyzed here are just a handful of poets – five to be precise – taken from five different geographical locations, but the themes they evoke are common to that of poetry written by women the world over as they share some common affinities with women as different as the Australian poet Judith Wright or the Italian Sibilla Aleramo or the Chilean Gabriella Mistral.

The subject stretches into infinity and merits further pursuit. The present collection of essays is, in this respect, an initial foray into a more extended study.

Bibliography

Akhmatova, Anna. *The Complete Poems of Anna Akhmatova,* V. I & II, tr. Judith Hemschemeyer. Somerville, MA: Zephyr Press, 1990.

Atwood, Margaret. "The Curse of Eve or What I have learned at School," *Women on Women*, ed. Ann B. Sheteir. The Gertstein Lecture Series. New York: New York University Press, 1978.

Atwood, Margaret. *Power Politics*. Toronto: Anansi, 1971.

Atwood, Margaret. *Survival: a Thematic Guide to Canadian Literature*. Toronto: Anansi, 1972.

Atwood, Margaret. *Second Words*. Toronto: Anansi, 1982.

Barbera, Jack, and William McBrien. *Stevie: A Biography of Stevie Smith*. New York: Oxford University Press, 1985.

Berlin, Isaiah. "Anna Akhmatova: A Memoir," in Hemschemeyer, ed. 24-45.

Brewster, Anne. "The Freedom to Decompose: The Poetry of Kamala Das," *Journal of Indian Writing in English*, VIII, 1-2, July 1980.

Browning, Elizabeth Barrett. *Sonnets from the Portuguese.* New York: Limited Editions Club, 1948.

Browning, Elizabeth Barrett. *Aurora Leigh.* Athens: Ohio University Press, 1992.

Buchbinder, David. "Weaving Her Version: The Homeric Model and Gender Politics in *Selected Poems*" in Van Spanckeren and Castro, 122-41.

Cixous, Helene. "The Laugh of the Medusa" in Courtivron and Marks.

Courtivron, Isabelle de, and Elaine Marks, eds. *New French Feminisms: An Anthology*. Amherst : University of Massachusetts Press, 1980.

Das, Kamala. *Collected Poems*. Trivandrum: n.p., 1984.

Das, Kamala. Interview: "I Needed to Disturb Society," in Iqbal Kaur, ed., *Perspectives on Kamala Das's Poetry*. 157-68.

Das, Kamala. *My Story*, New Delhi: Sterling Publishers, 1976.

Davies, Jessie. *Anna of All the Russias: The Life of Anna Akhmatova (1889-1996).* Liverpool: Lincoln Davies & Co., 1988.

Dick, Kay. *Ivy & Stevie: Ivy Compton-Burnett and Stevie Smith.* London: Duckworth, 1971.

Dickinson, Emily. *Final Harvest: Emily Dickinson's Poems* selected and introduced by Thomas H. Johnson. (Boston and Toronto: Little, Brown and Co., 1961).

Dickey, James. Review of *To Bedlam and Part Way Back*, in "First Five Books," *Poetry* 97 [Feb. 1961]: 318-319

George, Diana Hume, ed. *Sexton: Selected Criticism*. Urbana: U. of Illinois Press, 1988.

George, Diana Hume. *Oedipus Anne: The Poetry of Anne Sexton*. Urbana: U. of Illinois Press, 1987.

Haight, Amanda. *Anna Akhmatova: A Poetic Pilgrimage*. New York and London: Oxford University Press, 1976.

Hall, Caroline King Bernard. *Anne Sexton*. Boston: Twayne Publishers, 1989.

Harrex, S. C., and Vincent O'Sullivan, eds. *Kamala Das: A Selection with Essays on Her Work*. Adelaide: Center for Research in the New Literatures in English, 1986.

Hemschemeyer, Judith, tr. *The Complete Poems of Anna Akhmatova, V I & II.* Somerville, MA: Zephyr Press, 1990.

Juhasz, Suzanne. *Naked and Fiery Forms: Modern American Poetry by Women.* New York: Octagon, 1978.

Kevles, Barbara. "The Art of Poetry XV: Anne Sexton," *Paris Review* 13, no. 52 (summer 1971).

Kaur, Iqbal, ed. *Perspectives on Kamala Das's Poetry*. New Delhi: Intellectual Publishing House, 1995.

Kaur, Iqbal, ed. *Perspectives on Kamala Das's Prose*. New Delhi: Intellectual Publishing House, 1995.

Kaur, Iqbal. *Feminist Revolution and Kamala Das's* My Story. Patiala: Century Twentyone Publications, 1992.

Kohli, Devendra. *Kamala Das*. New Delhi: Arnold-Heinemann, Indian Writers Series, 1971.

MacGibbon, James, ed. *The Collected Poems of Stevie Smith*. London: Allen Lane, 1975.

McClatchy, J. D. *Anne Sexton: The Artist and Her Critics*. Bloomington: Indiana U. Press, 1978.

Millett, Kate. *Sexual Politics*. Garden City, New York: Doubleday, 1970.

Nabar, Vrinda. *The Endless Female Hungers: A Study of Kamala Das*. New Delhi: Sterling, 1994.

Naiman, Anatoly. "A Guest Upon the Earth," in Hemschemeyer, ed. 13-23.

Phillips, Robert. *The Confessional Poets*. Carbondale: Southern Illinois U. Press, 1973.

Rahman, Anisur. Expressive Form in the Poetry of Kamala Das. New Delhi: Abhinav Publications, 1981.

Ramakrishna, E. V. "Kamala Das as a Confessional Poet," Journal of Indian Writing in English, V. V, no. 1, Jan. 1977.

Rankin, Arthur C. *The Poetry of Stevie Smith: Little Girl Lost*. Gerrarda Cross, Bucks.: Colin Smythe, 1985.

Rich, Adrienne. "When We Dead Awaken," *On Lies, Secrets and Silence*. New York: W. W. Norton, 1969.

Rossetti, Christina. *Goblin Market*. London, Oxford University Press, 1913.

Rosslyn, Wendy. *The Prince, The Fool and the Nunnery: The Religious Theme in the Early Poetry of Anna Akhmatova*. Amersham, England: Avebury Publishing Co, 1984.

Sexton, Anne. *Anne Sexton: A Self-Portrait in Letters*, ed. Linda Grey Sexton. Boston: Houghton, 1977.

Sexton, Anne. *No Evil Star: Selected Essays, Interviews, and Prose*, ed. Steven E. Colburn. Ann Arbor: U. of Michigan Press, 1985.

Sexton, Anne. *The Complete Poems*. Boston: Houghton, 1981.

Showalter, Elaine. "Feminist Criticism in the Wilderness," in *The New Feminist Criticism* 243-270.

Showalter, Elaine. " The Feminist Critical Revolution," in *The New Feminist Criticism* 3-17.

Showalter, Elaine, ed. *The New Feminist Criticism: Essays on Women, Literature, and Theory*. New York: Pantheon Books, 1985.

Singh, Khushwant, ed. *Love and Friendship*. New Delhi: Sterling, 1973

Smith, Stevie. *Novel On Yellow Paper or Work It Out For Yourself*, with an introduction by Janet Watts. London: Virago, 1980.

Smith, Stevie. *The Collected Poems*. London: Penguin, 1985.

Spalding, Frances. *Stevie Smith*. London: Faber, 1988.

Sternlicht, Sanford, ed. *In Search of Stevie Smith*. Syracuse: Syracuse University Press, 1991.

Sternlicht, Sanford. *Stevie Smith*. Boston: Twayne, 1990.

Stevie Smith. *New Selected Poems*. New York: New Directions, 1988.

Subba Rao, M. *Readings in Indo-Anglian Literature: Prospective and Retrospective*. V.2. New Delhi: Kanishka Publishers, 1995.

Van Spanckeren, Kathryn, and Jan Garden Castro. *Margaret Atwood: Visions and Forms*. Carbondale : Southern Illinois University Press, 1988.

Wagner-Martin, Linda, ed. *Critical Essays on Anne Sexton*. Boston: G. K. Hall, 1989.